MEDIT

ON THE

LOVE OF GOD

TRANSLATED FROM THE SPANISH OF

FRAY DIEGO DE ESTELLA

BY

HENRY W. PEREIRA, M.A., M.R.I.A.

Nihil obstat.

    GULIELMUS L. GILDEA, S.T.D.,
        Censor deputatus.

Imprimatur.

    HERBERTUS CARDINALIS VAUGHAN,
        Archiepiscopus Westmonast.

Die 30 *Dec.,* 1898.

Diego de Estella, the author of the work from which the following pages have been translated, was born A.D. 1524, at Estella, in the Kingdom of Navarre. In due course he assumed the cowl of the Order of S. Francis, as one of the Friars Minor of the Regular Observance, at Salamanca.

He was appointed Royal Preacher, Adviser and Theologian to King Philip II., and became Confessor to Cardinal Granvela.

To his pen we owe, besides several works in Latin, the following written in Spanish: 1. *De la vanidad del mundo;* 2. *Meditaciones del Amor de Dios;* 3. *La vida y excelencias de san Juan Evangelista.*

The first of these works was one of the very few books recommended by Dona Oliva de Sabuco; the second is the subject of the present translation.

Diego died at Salamanca, 1st August, 1578, *ætat.* fifty-four.

H. W. P.

MEDITATIONS ON THE LOVE OF GOD.

MEDITATION I.

HOW ALL CREATION INVITES US TO THE LOVE OF GOD.

ALL Thy creatures declare to me, O Lord, that I should love Thee, and in every one of them I discover a tongue which proclaims Thy goodness and greatness. The beauty of the heavens, the brightness of the sun and moon, the effulgence of the stars, the splendour of the planets, the currents of the waters, the verdure of the fields, the diversity of flowers, the variety of colours, and all that Thy divine hands have made, O God of my heart and Spouse of my soul, tell me that I should love Thee. Everything that I see invites me to Thy love, and reproaches me when I love Thee not. I cannot open my eyes without beholding preachers of Thy most exalted wisdom! I cannot open my ears without hearing those who proclaim Thy goodness; for everything that Thou hast made tells me, O Lord, what Thou art.

All created things teach the love of the Creator rather than that of the creature which is His gift.

The Scripture saith, in speaking of the creation of the world, that the Spirit of God moved upon the waters; whence we understand that over all things hovered that Divine Spirit which sustains and governs them with gentle sway. Everything has its first source in the living fountain of love; and everything which continues to exist becomes tinctured with love: so that if the eyesight of our soul were not blinded by the worthlessness and vileness of its own passion and self-love, the principal thing which it would discover in all creation would be the love of the Creator.

Hence it is that Thy friends, O Lord, with greater ingenuity and more subtle art than that famous philosopher who taught men to produce fire from flint, are able to bring forth sparks of the fire of love out of every creature however insignificant. Thus, if the earth sustains me and supplies me with its fruits, Holy Love is the good and careful gardener who commanded it to do so when He created it. If the air refreshes me, and imparts new life, Love has so ordained it, for it could not do so of itself, as being merely a secondary cause. If the water is serviceable to us and supplies us with its fish and runs with great force to the sea, from whence it originated, all this is in order to fulfil the commandment of Love. Finally, if the fire gives forth heat; if the sky gives light and impulse, creating various metals in the earth, all is for my benefit and for the pleasure of the only friend whom this Infinite Love —our God—has created for Himself upon the earth.

What, O Lord, are the elements, the birds, animals, skies and planets, but burning coals with which Thou hast set fire to my frozen heart, in order to dispose it to love Him Whom so many gifts invite that heart to take as its rightful lover? What are the sun and the moon, the heavens and the earth, but jewels given by Thy hand to shadow forth to us Thy great beneficence and love? Every morning, my soul, thou findest at the door of thy house the whole universe, the birds, animals, fields and skies, which are waiting to serve thee, in order that thou mayest repay them all by that service of unconstrained love which thou owest in behalf of them all to thy Creator and theirs. All things call upon thee to awake to the love of thy God; and all, like a steward in behalf of his lord, set before thee the claim that there is upon thy love. To His love thou art invited by the great cry of all His creatures—as well the superior orders as the inferior—which with open voice declare to thee His majesty, His beauty and His greatness. "The heavens show forth the glory of God, and the firmament declareth the work of His hands: there are no speeches nor languages where their voices are not heard"[1]; so much so that all men are without excuse.

Even when silent, O Lord, the heavens show forth

[1] Ps. xviii. 2, 4; *cf.* Rom. i. 20.

Thy glory and declare to us how great must be the dwelling-place of Thy chosen ones, since Thou permittest the eyes of mortals to behold such beauty. O how rich must Thou be, my God, since Thou art attended by such glorious lights! From what design could such exquisite work proceed? Who could produce such beauteous brightness, such various influences, so many and such different movements, without an error in a single point? With good reason does Job inquire "Dost thou know the order of heaven, and canst thou set down the reason thereof on the earth?"[1]

O how glorious is the House of the Lord, and how boundless His dwelling-place! Behold Thy heavens, the works of Thy fingers, the moon and the stars which Thou hast founded.[2] Everything that my eyes discern tells me that I should love Thee. Then if I turn aside to the lesser world, which is man, and fix my eyes upon myself, I find there still greater reason for loving Thee, for Thou hast created all the aforesaid creatures for my service and benefit. If I open my ears I shall hear the Psalmist who says to me: "Thy knowledge is become wonderful to me".[3] From the knowledge of myself comes far higher wisdom in the knowledge of Thee. For this reason Thy prophet Isaias saith to sinners: "Remember this, and be ashamed; return, ye transgressors, to the heart".[4]

---

[1] Job xxxviii. 33. [2] Ps. viii. 4. [3] *Ibid.*, cxxxviii. 6. [4] Isa. xlvi. 8.

MEDITATION II.

HOW CREATED THINGS ATTRACT US TO THE DIVINE LOVE.

ALL that I behold with my eyes attracts me to Thee, my God and Lord; and all that Thou hast created helps me to understand Thy Divine greatness. As the arrow does not remain fixed in the air, but flies onward, so our reflections and thoughts are not intended to remain fixed upon the things of earth, but upon the end and the final resting-place, which is Thyself, my God. All those things which we see are like a road to lead us to consider the Creator. "The Spirit of the Lord hath filled the whole world; and that which containeth all things hath knowledge of the voice."[1] He is blind who is not enlightened by such splendour in created things; he is deaf who is not awakened by such sounds; he is dumb who, with such actualities around him, does not glorify God; and he is a fool who, with such evidences before him, does not discern the first principle and cause of all this.

Open thine eyes, then, my soul; apply thy spiritual

[1] Wisd. i. 7.

ears; loosen thy lips, and open thy heart, that thou mayest discern God in all His creatures, and mayest hearken to Him, praise, love and magnify Him: and so may not set the whole compass of the earth against thee. The compass of the earth fights against the foolish; while, on the contrary, it will prove a source of glory to the wise who can say with the prophet: "For Thou hast given me, O Lord, a delight in Thy doings; and in the works of Thy hands I shall rejoice".[1] "O how great are Thy works, O Lord; Thou hast made all things in wisdom; the earth is filled with Thy riches."[2] I behold in every created thing, as in a mirror, an evidence of Thy omnipotence, my God. The Majesty of the Creator shines forth in His creatures as in a glass. The senses are the door of the imagination, and by our senses we behold the creatures, through the knowledge of which we come to understand the goodness and wisdom of the Creator.

Ezechiel[3] when proposing to describe the building up of the Church begins with the outside wall. Before my soul ascends to the contemplation of the infinite perfections which Thou possessest in Thyself, my God, I must lift up my heart to Thy holy love, being attracted by those outward things which I see with my eyes, since they elevate me to the knowledge of Thee. "Woe unto you who regard not the work of the Lord, nor do you consider the operation of His

---

[1] Ps. xci. 5.   [2] *Ibid.*, ciii. 24.   [3] Ezech. xi. 5, etc.

hands,"[1] saith Thy holy prophet Isaias. Very often by their works are the masters who have wrought them known, although we do not behold them with our bodily eyes. The statues of Phidias the celebrated sculptor demonstrated what he was, and those who had never beheld him yet knew him in this way; while Protogenes likewise recognised the great painter Apelles by a single line which he had drawn.

O Creator of all things, what is there that is so clear an image of what Thou art as myself? What more subtle and delicate lines could the hand of any artist or any clever and very excellent painter execute which could approach or be compared with the surpassing and extreme beauty of the splendours of the sky and the flowers of the field?

Then if we regard the order, harmony and concord of this universe, what canst thou say, my soul, but that thou art lifted up and made to hang upon thy God? It is a harmony so complete, with such admirable unity and proportion, that if thou wert not deaf, it would make thee forget every created thing, thy whole self being transfused into thy Creator. Each string of the instrument sounds sweetly, but all united produce a delicious melody. Every creature by itself represents to me Thy infinite power and unspeakable goodness; but when all are contemplated together, and while we regard the order

[1] Isa. v. 12.

of the universe, they contribute to excite an extraordinary admiration.

When the skilful musician tunes into order the discordant and diverse strings of his instrument, although you do not see him, you judge him to be great in his art. If, my soul, thou regardest the entire creation, thou wilt find marvellous harmony in things contrary to each other, since the elements, while they contain conflicting qualities, do not fight against each other, nor do lowly things run counter to the higher ones; but all unite in concord, and produce a harmony of most admirable proportion and unity, the hand of the infinite wisdom of thy God being their moving impulse.

This Lord, holding the universe as an instrument of music, unites heavenly with earthly things, general with individual. While taking note of this diversity of things so well ordered, I reflect within myself on those words of the wise man, who says: "Let them know how much the Lord of them is more beautiful than they; for the first Author of beauty made all those things".[1] O how much more beautiful must He be Who hath made all things, for the Author of beauty hath painted all! O what must be the Providence of Him Who forecasts so fully for such a multitude of things, as if He were God for one only! From whence are extracted the varied tints of plants,

---

[1] "Quorum si specie delectati deos putaverunt, sciant quanto his dominator eorum speciosior est," etc. Sapient xiii. 3 (Vulg.).

the sweetness of fruits, the colours of birds, and the loveliness of the world? O how mighty must He be Who created all this out of nothing, and how wise He Who bestowed so many different instincts on animals, so many properties on roots, so many virtues on plants, and such various powers of genius on men; all which, when combined together, is, in comparison with Him, as if it did not exist!

Raise thyself up, then, my soul; open thine eyes and wake up; and if thou canst not discern the Divine virtue which wrought these things, at least pay regard to the works themselves, since they plainly declare Who made them, in order that He might be *known*, Who yet cannot be comprehended. For this cause Thou, O Lord, saidst to certain blind persons who, even when they had Thee before them, did not know Thee: "Though ye will not believe Me, believe the works".[1] Those works declared Who Thou wert; if they who saw Thee had only had eyes to consider them; for it was no more possible to consider them and not to know Thee, than it is possible to know Thee and fail to love Thee.

[1] S. John x. 38.

MEDITATION III.

THAT GOD IS TO BE LOVED FOR HIMSELF.

IT betrays a most consummate perversity to delight in those things which we are simply intended to use, and only to make use of those which we ought to enjoy. To enjoy is to love a thing for its own sake; to use it is to desire it not for itself, but for the sake of something else. He is evil who merely uses the Creator and enjoys the creature. He loves God not for Himself, but out of regard for other things, and for the benefits which he hopes for from Him, while he loves the creature for its own sake. Such a one is a transgressor of the law, and perverts the order of love. He is unworthy of God who loves his own things better than God.

Love has its proper end; and that which is its final object is that which we truly love; while we merely *use* all other means, not loving them for themselves, but because they are the means which are provided in order to attain the final end that we desire, and wherein our love becomes tranquil and at rest.

What greater wrong, then, canst thou do to thy God, O my soul, than by loving His gifts more than the very Creator Himself? If thou love not God for Himself, but for that which He bestows upon thee, and for what thou hopest from Him, dost not thou prefer and esteem the gift more than the Giver? The wife does a wrong to her husband when she loves the jewels and presents of her husband more than himself.

There are many men who love others, not for their riches, or their favours, or for the goods which they possess, since those who love have a greater abundance of such things than the objects of their regard; but they love them for their goodness, and for their pleasant and sweet conversation. Why, then, O Lord, should I not act towards Thee as one man does towards another, in loving Thee for what Thou art, without seeking my own interest? I love Thee as much as I am able, and to the utmost that is possible for me; and yet, with all this, I am dissatisfied with the small amount of my affection for Thee; since I should require to possess infinite power to be able to love Thee without limit.

If by any impossible chance it fell to my choice either to be placed in glory rejoicing in the vision of Thy Divine Essence, after having offended Thee; or to burn in hell, suffering all the pains which the damned endure, while still near Thee, I would rather be tormented in the deepest pit of hell, while retaining Thy Divine grace, than rejoice in Thy glory whilst Thou wert angry with me. My glory is to satisfy Thee, and my hell is to have Thee displeased with me.

Grant me, O Lord, Thy grace, and deal with me as Thou wilt. Give me Thy holy love, and dispose of me according to Thy will; which, even if I have to suffer all the torments of hell, would be to me as if I were in Paradise, so long as I serve Thee there and do Thy will. If I turn away in horror from that unhappy place, it is not so much on account of the punishment that I dread it as because I know that those who dwell there are Thy enemies; and if I love eternal blessedness and heavenly glory, I do not desire it so much for my own gratification and delight, as because I know that those who there rejoice in Thee are Thy friends, and are assured and very certain that they can never offend Thee.

This only does my soul desire, that it should never displease Thee, and that it should ever persevere in Thy holy love. Make me but secure of Thy friendship, for it is enough for me to have Thee near me to be sure that I should never be sorrowful, nor receive annoyance through anything that could happen to me. I only desire Thee, only love Thee; my greatest bliss is to draw near to Thee, and this alone suffices me.

O how gentle is Thy Spirit, O Lord! how sweet Thy converse! and how worthy art Thou of being loved for Thyself! He is a slave and the vilest hireling who seeks any other thing than Thee. Is Thy being the highest good and infinite beneficence so small a thing that Thou dost not deserve to be loved except for what Thou possessest and canst bestow upon us? O what a wrong does he commit against Thee who only serves Thee and keeps Thy commandments, not so much from love of Thee, nor because Thou commandest him, as for his own private benefit!

In the book of Deuteronomy after Moses had said that we ought to love Thee, he adds: "And these words which I command thee this day shall be in thy heart".[1] Herein he gives us to understand that the cause and principal reason why we ought to love Thee is because Thou commandest and desirest it. Not merely for the blessings which we hope for from Thee, nor because Thou dost threaten with punishment those who love Thee not, but most chiefly because Thou commandest it, and because it is Thy will that we should love Thee. By whom does a father desire his work to be done but by the son who possesses love for him? For whom dost Thou, my God, desire glory but for those who love Thee? Thy Apostle saith: "That eye hath not seen, nor ear heard, nor hath it entered into the heart of man what things God hath prepared for them that love Him".[2] For those who love Thee, O Lord, Thou

---

[1] Deut. vi. 6.   [2] 1 Cor. ii. 9.

hast Thy blessedness laid up in store; and those sons who serve Thee for love's sake shall enter into it.

He who seeks Thee only is able to find Thee, and with Thee shall possess all good things. Thee only do I love and desire, and Thou only art the reward of all my labours, according to that which Thou saidst to the patriarch Abraham: "I am thy reward exceeding great".[1] Thou art that most abundant and full reward of which David speaks when addressing Thee in the psalm: "I have inclined my heart to do Thy justifications for ever, for the reward".[2] Thou, my soul, oughtest to love freely Him Who gratuitously purchased thee, giving the price of thy redemption, without which thou couldst not have deserved to be redeemed. Thou shouldst not desire to seek anything further, since He alone is sufficient for thee.

However covetous thou mayest be, thou oughtest to be content with Him only. Although thy covetousness may desire to possess heaven and earth, He is much more Who made both the heavens and the earth. In Him alone thou wilt possess all that thou canst desire, and all that thou canst claim. "Forgive Thy people, O Lord,"

---

[1] Gen. xv. 1.

[2] Ps. cxviii. 112. From the Vulgate, which follows the LXX. δι' ἀντάμειψιν, instead of the Hebrew עֵקֶב, *i.e.*, *usque ad finem*. The passage is correctly rendered in the translation of Cipriano de Valera: "Mi corazon incliné à poner por obra tus estatutos de continuo, *hasta el fin*".

said Moses to God, "or blot me out of the Book of Life."[1] Moses did not desire to be separated from the love of God, but he so loved God and his neighbours that for the love of them he was willing to be deprived of that glory which was to his own advantage and interest; being satisfied with the love of God alone.

[1] Exod. xxxii. 32.

MEDITATION IV.

THAT GOD IS TO BE LOVED AS BEING SUPREMELY GOOD.

IF the object of our desire is the true, the sublimest, and the highest good, why should not my heart love Thee above all things, since Thou art supremely good, and beneficence itself? It is impossible for man to love anything if it be not either really good, or at least presented under the colour and pretence of good. When he loves what is evil, he does not desire it in so far as it is evil, but because the evil comes to him concealed under cover of some good, by which the will, being excited, is carried away by mistake to wish for the evil, which would never be loved by our will if it came to us undisguised.

The world presents to our choice things apparently good, such as its pleasures, honours, temporal advantages and other like things. But beneath such transitory and defective good comes death, together with the abominations of various vices and sins. Thou submittest to these deceits, my soul, when—devoting thyself to these outward vanities—thou purchasest eternal and lasting torments at the price of losing thy freedom. Canst thou not see that it is falsehood and wickedness to forsake thy God, Who is supremely good, and a pure act of beneficence, for a goodness so superficial as that which displays itself in the creature?

The goodness of the creature is only a tiny drop which flows from that boundless ocean and profound illimitable abyss of the ineffable goodness of the Creator. Why then dost thou abandon the reality for a mere appearance, and that which is truly good for a mere shadow of goodness? Beneath this trivial goodness which thou seest in creatures, and which they have received as a gift from the exceeding goodness of the Creator, are hidden many imperfections; but the goodness of the Lord is His own proper attribute, without the admixture of any imperfection.

What wickedness then is it on thy part to forsake that which is substantially and essentially good and so worthy of being loved for the sake of a little transient good which covers many defects and faults that are only deserving of abhorrence! "None is good, save God only," saith the Scripture; for He alone is substantially good, and His goodness is natural to Him and a property of His essence; but the goodness of the creature is acquired, communicated, borrowed and very superficial, and is not good in itself, except by participating in the goodness which it received from God.

My God, Who art the source and spring from whence proceeds all the goodness that I love on earth, let my heart love Thee above all things, since according to its natural instinct it cannot be lifted up except by that which is good, nor taken captive except by excellence real or apparent. O Lord, Who art the supreme excellence and the true good, I ought to love Thee, for Thou art altogether good, and the chief object of my heart; Thou art the end of my desires, the repose of my mind, and the fulfilment of my wishes. Thou art essentially good, and all other goodness is something merely subsidiary, and unworthy of having my love occupied with it.

Thou didst command Thy servant Moses[1] to make "a mercy-seat" or "propitiatory" (for the sacred ark), which was a large and lofty altar of pure and massive gold without any sculptured device, which was set above the ark of the covenant between the Cherubim who looked into it, and from whence Thou gavest Thy responses. If, as Thy holy apostle saith, all the ceremonies of that law were figures of the law of grace, what did that altar of pure and solid gold represent but Thy pure, solid, substantial and true goodness? In us goodness is like tinsel, which is fitted on our persons over many weaknesses and defects: but in Thee it is all fine gold, because Thou art essentially altogether good.

A pictured device is a thing entirely accidental and external, and for this reason Thou didst command that the altar should not be sculptured; for in Thee there

[1] Exod. xxv. 17, 18.

is nothing accidental, nor is that goodness a mere casual quality, which belongs to Thee by reason of Thine own Nature. The altar was large and wide, for Thy great goodness extends to those that are without, even to the unbelieving and enemies. The sun arises upon the good and bad; and Thou rainest upon the just and the unjust.[1] Thou didst not reject the thief who cried unto Thee upon the cross;[2] Thou didst not despise the sinful woman who sought Thee in the house of the Pharisee;[3] nor didst Thou hide Thyself from the adulteress whom they set before Thee in the Temple;[4] and Thou didst not disdain to receive sinners and to eat with them, notwithstanding the murmuring of the Pharisees.[5] Thou wast not an accepter of persons; nor did any sinner, however great, come to Thee without finding those bowels of love opened for his relief.

O how ample and widely extended is Thy beneficence, most merciful Lord, for Thou embracest the poor and the slave, the vile and wretched serf, and the miserable sinner, as well as the great, powerful and rich, equally with him who is very high in Thy service! The Cherubim remained gazing upon and contemplating the mercy-seat; for it is an understood truth that only the

[1] S. Matt. v. 45.   [2] S. Luke xxiii. 42, 43.
[3] *Ibid.*, vii. 47.   [4] S. John viii. 11.
[5] S. Luke xv. 2.

angelic and human natures can know Thee, and only angels and men take notice of Thy infinite goodness. They held their wings outstretched, because in the consideration and contemplation of Thy goodness our desires are enkindled, and the soul stretches out its affections, ascending with its holy devotions and fervent sighs, loving above all things the will of Him Whom the understanding knows to be worthy of being loved above them all.

Everything that men love is loved for the sake of some good which it possesses; wherefore the good itself is more worthy of being loved. O Lord, since Thou art goodness itself by reason of Thy beneficence, Thou art deserving of being supremely loved. "I will love Thee, O Lord, my strength; the Lord is my firmament, my refuge, and my deliverer."[1] Thou art greater in Thyself than in all that Thou hast done for us, and so it is right that my heart should love Thee for Thy infinite goodness, even more than for what Thou hast done for me.

Thou oughtest, then, my soul, to bathe thyself in this boundless ocean of the goodness of thy God, and to enter into the profound abyss of the supreme excellence of thy Creator. Let my heart burn in this flaming furnace of Thy boundless love, my God, and let my bowels be inflamed with the love of Thy eternal and sovereign goodness. I will love Thee, my God, Thou infinite good, Thou ineffable blessed-

[1] Ps. xvii. 2, 3.

ness, Who art love without measure or limit, with all my power, and above all things: for Thou art the supreme Good, and the fountain from whence flow forth the benefits which all other things contain.

MEDITATION V.

THAT GOD IS TO BE LOVED AS BEING OF SURPASSING BEAUTY.

IF beauty has such power to take captive the desires, why, O my heart, art thou not captivated by this infinite beauty of thy Creator? O fountain of all beauty, from which all other beauties flow, why am I not wholly transported by the consummate perfection of such extreme and sovereign comeliness? The beauty of created things is trivial, transitory, momentary and perishable. To-day it is fresh as the flower of the field, and on the morrow it is withered away. The beauty of the creature fades, and fails to continue any great length of time; but the beauty of the Creator endures for ever, and is coexistent with Himself.

All beauty compared with that of the Lord is very great deformity. Why, then, O my soul, dost thou suffer thyself to be possessed by a love of the deformity existing in the deceitful creature, which is covered with a false appearance of beauty, whilst thou forsakest the true beauty of thy God? The beauty of the Creator has greater superiority over that of the creature than the substance over the shadow. Since, then, the shadow that thou lovest allures thee so strongly, why does not the light that thou desirest captivate thee?

If those works cause thee such admiration, which yet cannot be impressed with the perfection which they possess in the divine pattern, on account of the dulness of the material whereon they have been elaborated, how is it that thou art not transported beyond thyself when contemplating the beauty and perfection which exist in the pattern from which they were derived? What man can there be in the world who, having been inspired with a great admiration for a very beautiful likeness of a person drawn from nature, does not become much more attached to the individual person?

If, then, all creatures are Thy handiwork, my God, and man is Thy image and likeness, why, O Lord, am I not more inspired with affection for Thee than for Thine image and likeness? And if I love with such regard things whose value lies chiefly in the fact that they are coveted by me, why should I not love Him without Whom there is no good whatever, and Who created those very things out of love for me?

My heart shall be taken captive by the infinite beauty of my God. O beauty of such long standing, yet so new, how slow have I been in learning to know Thee, how late in loving Thee! Art not Thou, O Lord, peradventure, the very One of Whom the Psalmist declares: "Thou art beautiful above the sons of men"?[1] Of Thee the Bride affirms that Thou art "White and ruddy, chosen out of thousands".[2]

And if in this place of exile I do not discern the beauty of Thy Divine Majesty as Thou art beautiful in heaven, yet through the beauty of the heavens, the planets, trees, flowers, and the variety of the very vivid colours in those things which Thy Divine Hands have made, I know my God and Lord to be an infinite abyss of beauty, even of that beauty from which these other beauties derive their origin.

Therefore, if in this world we can in any degree take note of Thy Divine beauty, which is the beginning and cause of all that is beautiful, why does not the knowledge thus acquired by my judgment and reason carry me away with impetuous haste, and exalt me to the love of such great perfection and beauty? The brave apparel[3] of the beautiful Judith captivated the Prince Holofernes; the beauty of Esther changed the iron heart of Assuerus into tenderness.[4] How is it, then, that I do not forget myself and all things in the world for the love of Thy infinite beauty?

The Scripture pronounces ephemeral beauty to be

---

[1] Ps. xliv. 3.   [2] Cant. v. 10.
[3] See Judith x. 3 *seq.*; xii. 15, and xvi. 8, 9.
[4] Esther ii. 15.

mere vanity,[1] in order the more effectually to mock him who loves it. But this eternal beauty, which is peculiar to Thee, my God, will endure as long as Thou endurest, which will be for ever without end. Jonas refreshed himself beneath the verdure of the ivy,[2] which being gnawed by a worm soon withered away. Decay and foul corruption are inseparably united to all corporeal beauty such as is that of the creature.

To what, then, can my soul have recourse, and wherewith can my love fill its heart, but with that everlasting and infinite beauty, which never dies and never decays? If from short-sightedness in this transitory life I cannot discern Thy beauty with my bodily eyes, it is enough that with the spectacles of faith I can attain to the knowledge thereof, by which consideration my soul and all my faculties are transfused into Thee, transported to the love of Thy ineffable beauty.

Great is the power which corporeal beauty possesses to excite the eyes, and through them to carry away the heart; and still greater is the dulness and stolid heaviness of him who can resolve to turn aside his heart to some corporeal beauty, while he has present before him a beauty so immeasurable as Thine, my God, which compels even Thine inanimate creatures to imitate it.

---

[1] Prov. xxxi. 30.

[2] "La verdura de la *yedra* verde": ivy; derived from the Vulgate, "hedera".

MEDITATION VI.

HOW GOD IS TO BE LOVED.

IF thou desirest, O my soul, to know the measure which thou must adopt in loving thy God, it is *without* measure. When He commanded thee to love thy neighbour, He set before thee a certain rate or proportion, saying that thou shouldst love him as thyself, and not more than thyself. But in commanding thee to love His Divine Majesty, He assigned no limits, but rather declared without restriction that thou shouldst love Him, because God is to be loved to the very utmost extent that thou canst love.

O Lord, Thou art so good, that however much Thy creature may love Thee, it can never love Thee as much as Thou deservest to be loved, and for this reason the measure wherewith it should love Thee is to love Thee without measure. So saith the Scripture: "Glorify the Lord as much as ever you can, for He will yet far exceed, and His magnificence is wonderful".[1] Love thy God, then, my soul, as much as He is capable of being loved, and this will be sufficient for thee. Why art thou

[1] Ecclus. xliii. 32.

surprised at what I say to thee? Perhaps thou knowest not that the Scripture commands us to praise Him according to the excellency of His greatness.[1]

Thou wilt tell me that no one can love Him in this manner except Himself, nor praise Him either; for He Himself alone can be equal to so loving Himself, Whose love is infinite as is His greatness also. Thou sayest well; but if thou canst not praise Him sufficiently, thou art not to cease from praising Him; and if thou canst not love Him as thou oughtest, love as much as thou canst, for thou hast no reason to fear excess or superfluity in love, where the faculty and the power is far surpassed by the glory and excellence of the person loved; and where the power of the lover and the eloquence of him who praises are exceeded by the worth and merit of the person praised.

The seraphs burn, and the angelic powers are inflamed with love towards Him, as it is written: "Who maketh His angels spirits and His ministers a burning fire".[2] They never cease from this ardent love, because it never seems to them that it is fervent enough. And what is all the love of this world compared with the fervour and flame of those angelic spirits and blessed souls? All our love is a great lukewarmness if it be compared with the fragrance and glow of these beings.

[1] Ps. cl. 2.   [2] *Ibid.*, ciii. 4.

I love Thee, then, my God and my Lord, without measure or limit, because in this manner hast Thou loved us; and Thou, Who hast made all things with weight, number and measure, hast in the exercise of Thy love, set neither measure nor bounds to it. In this way alone, O our God, Thou hast exceeded all measure, transcended all order, and surpassed all reason and understanding; and while preserving order in all things from the beginning, in loving us Thou hast not cared to preserve any method or order, but hast been beyond all bounds most bounteous and exuberant.

Pardon, I beseech Thee, O Lord, pardon Thy servant who speaketh thus of Thee with joy and great boldness, for Thou wast bountiful, most bountiful in loving us, O our God. Was it not beneficent beyond measure that the Son of God was hung upon the cross for a vile worm? Is it not a great extremity of love that the Creator should die, in order that the creature might live? Is it not a strange and excessive instance of love that the Maker should lose His life for the work which He had made, and the innocent for the guilty, the just for the sinner? If this, O Lord, is a measure, it is a measure with reference to Thy wisdom; for in respect to all created intelligences, this is extreme, a very great extreme, and exceeding bountifulness.

In danger we naturally put up the hand and arm to defend the head, which is the principal member of the body; but it was an excessive evidence of Thy great love that Thou, my God and Lord, being our Head, didst place Thyself in danger of death, and didst die upon the cross, in order to shelter us, Thy members. And so likewise Thy holy apostle, filled with the Spirit, was not afraid to say that the love wherewith Thou lovedst us was excessive,[1] in that being the Son of God Thou gavest Thyself for certain vile and despised slaves.

O truly excessive and very great love, which transcends the bounds of all love! The work of our redemption the prophet calls "plentiful redemption,"[2] but the apostle more properly entitles it exceeding and beneficent. Thy love was exceeding great, since in Thy Passion Thou didst pay for us more than we owed. Even an excessive satisfaction, inasmuch as one drop of Thy Blood would have sufficed for our atonement by reason of the infinite nature of the individual victim, whereas Thou gavest it all, showing the exceeding great love which Thou hadst for us.

It is thus that I am to love Thee, my God, as exceedingly, as truly, and as resolutely, so that there should be neither bounds nor measure in my love. I will go forth of myself and out of myself, loving Thee without being in myself, inebriated with this

---

[1] Ephes. ii. 4, 7. τὸν ὑπερβάλλοντα πλοῦτον τῆς χάριτος αὐτοῦ.
[2] Ps. cxxix. 7.

Thy holy love, and transported out of myself; for if love be genuine, it must harass[1] a man out of himself, because love surprises and creates ecstasy.

On this account the Bridegroom in the Song of Songs, while pondering on his love for the Bride, compares it to wine,[2] because of the property which wine possesses of transporting him who drinks much of it out of himself, and the Bride says to him: "The king brought me to his banqueting house" [The king "brought me into the cellar of wine," and "he set in order charity in me"];[3] and because he was speaking of love in referring to this wine, he added immediately after, "and he inclined my will to various degrees of love"

The soul when wounded will be able to extricate itself in the grace of forgiveness and endurance of injuries; but this is very easy and very lovely, in consideration of the employment in which Thy love has exercised itself. O my God, my infinite good! one ought to have the wisdom of the angels, in order to declare this thoughtfulness of Thine in our behalf! I am sure that whoever was well instructed in this matter would be perfectly enamoured of Thy Divine majesty and goodness. Thou didst set Thy love on the cross; and on the gall and vinegar; ours is fixed rather on honeycombs.

---

[1] Literally, draw or tease a man out of the points or houses of a backgammon board.

[2] Cant. i. 1.   [3] *Ibid.*, ii. 4.

O what a hard law was that in our behalf, my God; and how sweet and easy is ours in respect to Thee! since even in dying Thou dost not fully fill up the law of Thy love, while even in living in Thy kingdom and glory we cannot fill up as we ought the law of our love. But so far as I am able and it may be possible for me I must love Thee in this life more than my own interests and more than myself. For this reason Thou didst ask Thy Apostle Saint Peter whether he loved Thee more than the others,[1] because Thou desirest to be loved by us more than all other things, and above them all, without limit and without measure. All other virtues admit of a measure and degree, but only the virtue of love and charity does not permit it.

[1] S. John xxi. 15.

MEDITATION VII.

HOW GOD ALONE IS TO BE LOVED.

LOVE is the feet of the soul, and I am carried by love whithersoever I wish to go; and as this body of ours possesses two feet with which it walks, so the soul has two loves and affections which carry it on, *viz.*, Thy Divine and holy love, and the love of worldly things. After Jacob had wrestled with the angel and was entitled the man who had seen God [face to face],[1] the angel touched him on one leg and made him lame of one foot.

O Lord, my soul in learning the excellence of Thy goodness, and in discovering somewhat of Thy Divine perfections, immediately goes halting in respect to the love of the world, and walks straight along the way of Thy holy love. Why should my soul become an adulteress when she has a husband so lovely and rich, and so worthy of being loved? I will be lame in the love of the world and the way of wickedness in order to walk lightly along the paths of Thy Divine love, when I shall have tasted of Thy sweetness, according

[1] Gen. xxxii. 30.

to what the prophet says when speaking to Thee: "I have run the way of Thy commandments when Thou didst enlarge my heart".[1]

Unfold the innermost membrane of my heart, fill it with the joy of love, that I may run with delight to keep Thy commandments. The burden of the love of the world weighs down the wings of my love, so that it cannot fly to Thee, my God, Who art the centre of my soul. Why should I desire to burden myself with the love of things which impede the flight of my soul to its Creator and Spouse? I will abhor from my heart everything beside Thee, since Thou alone art sufficient for me.

He loves Thee but little, O Lord, who loves other things together with Thee, if he does not love them for Thy sake. The love is severed, and the heart is divided in the case of the man who, not content with Thy love alone, loves the creatures, yet not for Thy sake. It is a marvellous thing that, man being what he is, Thou, my God, contentest Thyself with him alone; and that, being what Thou art, man is not satisfied with Thee alone, but seeks to love other things together with Thee, yet not for Thy sake, as if Thou only wert not sufficient for him. How couldst Thou, my God and my perfect good, be so small a thing to me that Thou shouldst not suffice for me?

O centre of my heart and Spouse of my soul! whom do I desire in heaven or earth but Thee?[2] If Thou

---

[1] Ps. cxviii. 32. [2] *Ibid.*, lxxii. 25 (not exact).

art goodness itself, and containest in a pre-eminent degree all good things, why doth my soul go forth to seek for good things in miserable creatures, and abandon Thee, the fountain of all goodness? Why doth my heart set out in search of the love of the creatures when experience has taught me that they cannot give me rest, and that I cannot find true repose in them? They themselves tell me that I should love Thee alone. I hold them in much esteem until I have obtained them, and after they are secured, they are counted as valueless.

Before they were obtained they had this virtue, that by their absence they had the power to move my desire with the appearance of good which was, however, more fallacious than real; but, after they were possessed, that desire ceased, and when the desire died away their slight value disclosed itself, and thus they are made of very little account. The more the creature is possessed, the better it is known; and when it is absent, it is unknown: by possession it discovers itself, and by discovering itself it exhibits those defects which were not known before, and thus the will holds it (the creature) in less esteem than before.

Earthly goods very soon become distasteful,[1] and when we begin to enjoy them they mortify us by their imperfections and defects. If then, Thou my God, the more Thou art possessed and loved, dost

---

[1] Literally, "strike us in the face".

more fully discover the riches of Thy goodness and Thy infinite perfections, why should I desire to weave a garment of wool and linen contrary to the law,[1] mingling the imperfect love of the creature with the excellency of Thy holy love?

The creature, if it gratifies me in some respects, does not care to do so in everything; and even if it were entirely desirous, it could not; and if it were both willing and able to do so wholly (which is impossible), it could not accomplish this in every place, nor at all times. Why then should I not prefer to be loved by One Who can gratify me in more things than I can either know, or think, or desire, or ask; and this in all places and at all times?

O how the world and our own flesh hold us bewitched; and how do we, in consequence, cease to love that eternal goodness and admirable beauty of God, in order to debase ourselves to things so vile as the creatures of this world!

All creatures are telling me, Love thy God and not me. Why dost thou love me? Wherefore dost thou desire me? Behold I am but earth and dust. What dost thou see in me that is not alien? Love only Him Who created us out of nothing, and Who bestowed upon us all that we are. Take heed that I do not deceive thee: for all that thou lovest in me, and all that thou seekest and desirest and that appears good

[1] Deut. xxii. 11.

to thee, is false. Remember that if thou love me I will slay thee, and will cause thy death. I am not designed for any other end than to lift up thy heart that thou mayst love thy Creator and mine.

The more beautiful the creature is, and the more the sense of love stirs thee, so much the more shouldst thou be inflamed with the love of thy Lord. If, then, my soul, thou lovest these temporal things, for the beauty which thou beholdest in them, much more oughtest thou to love thyself, since thou surpassest all that is earthly in elegance and perfection. If thou couldst discern the beauty of thy countenance, thou wouldst clearly understand how worthy of reproof thou art in thinking that there is anything external to thee which is worthy of thy love.

If, therefore, love cannot exist in solitude, and when it passes out of itself must love something else, whom oughtest thou to love but thy refuge and protector, Who is thy God, since everything corporeal is less than thyself? He wrongs himself who fixes his affection on things which are not worthy of him. It is expedient that every one should consider himself, and after he has understood his dignity, should not love things which are inferior to himself, that he may not do injury to his love. For those things which are beautiful when considered by themselves, become depreciated when compared with others more beautiful.

And as it is folly to unite ugly things with

those which are beautiful, so it is unbecoming to treat those things which have only an inferior show of beauty on an equality with those which are perfect and complete in their loveliness. If thou, my soul, dost not desire to retain thy love in solitude, thou shouldst not desire to keep it low and mean. If thou desire one only love, seek Him Who is to be loved alone. Thou knowest that love is fire, and that fire requires materials whereby it may burn; take care therefore that thou love not things which will only repay thee with smoke.

Take note of thy beauty, and thou wilt understand what beauty thou oughtest to love. All the world is subject to thee; and thou dost not disdain to admit to thy love—I do not say all the world, but some little particle of the world which in its nature is not beautiful, nor is a necessary element of good, nor extensive in quantity, nor very perfect in goodness. If thou love these things, love them as the gifts of thy God, fixing all thy love in thy Creator and its own. Love not the gifts which He bestows on thee more than the kindness of Him Who loves thee.

Thou doest a greater wrong to His love if, while receiving His benefits, thou dost not pay thy love in the same coin by loving Him Who loveth thee. Undervalue His gifts if thou canst; but if thou canst not scorn them, pay Him back with the same love. Thou art unworthy of the love of thy God, if thou set thy love on these transitory things. Love Him, and love thyself for the love of Him; love His gifts for His sake, love Him because thou hast joy in Him, and love thyself because thou art loved by Him.

MEDITATION VIII.

HOW GOD IS TO BE LOVED AS BEING THE CENTRAL OBJECT OF OUR SOUL.

ALL things naturally seek their centre, and desire their perfection and end, and therein they rest and are quieted. The stone seeks its natural centre, and therefore falls. The rivers flow towards the sea from whence they issued; and thus they move onwards with great impetus in order to reach their proper place. Fire mounts up rapidly to its own sphere, and does not cease to do so until it attains its ultimate end. O Creator of our souls! what art Thou but their centre and end? Thou hast created us for the purposes of Thy love, and our heart is restless until it attain to Thee.

As the stone is inclined to fall to the centre, so my soul desires the *Summum Bonum* which Thou art, my God; and as the stone, forced out of its centre, when the impediment which obstructed it is removed immediately falls down, so my soul is never quiet nor hushed to rest until it attain to Thee. My soul finds no rest in riches, nor in honours, nor in pleasures, but only in Thee, my God, the true rest and repose of my heart.

This was what the Wise Man reflected when he said: "Vanity of vanities, all is vanity".[1] Vain is everything which does not fill up some place; and vain therefore are all those earthly things, since they do not supply the capacities of the soul, nor satisfy its longings, nor are they of a character to gratify its desires.

If, then, all things naturally proceed towards their end, and Thou, O Lord, art the end of man, and the most perfect of all things, it is right that we should make progress toward Thee, with greater impetus and speed than that with which other things in nature move towards their centre and to their own individual ends. And whereas the feet upon which my soul draws nigh to Thee are its affections, it is necessary that I should love Thee, my God, in order to attain to my centre.

Thou callest us to this repose and peace, O Lord, when Thou sayest in Thy holy gospel, "Come to Me, all you that labour and are burdened, and I will refresh you".[2] Ye go on your way restless and disquieted, serving the world and your own passions: come unto Me, and ye will then be in your proper sphere, enjoying quiet and repose.

Break away, then, my soul, more truly from the world, and abandoning its heavy burdens, return to thy rest: for it is very clear, if thou wilt only open thine eyes, that the power of love will

---

[1] Eccles. i. 2.   [2] S. Matt. xi. 28.

lift thee up to thy Lord as to thy proper centre. Thou art very sensible that thou hast no rest outside of Him; wherefore when thou art with Him, then thou shalt be at rest, and shalt say with the prophet: "In peace in the self-same I will sleep and I will rest;"[1] and if thou wilt appeal to the experience which thou hast had it will tell thee that thy love can find no rest but in God, for all other things project thee out of themselves and send thee to thy centre.

Seest thou not clearly that if thou lovest anything outside of God, in such love there is great disquietude and bitterness and deadly anguish? Oh how insipid, how bitter, and how full of anguish is every creature if it be loved for itself! What tragedies and what mournful and lamentable occurrences do foolish lovers relate to us on this subject if we desire to question them! They would never come to an end in telling them nor we in listening to them.

Every creature casts thee away from itself with ignominy and insults thee in order that by detaching thyself from it thou mightest succeed in drawing near to thy Creator, as if contumeliously addressing thee it said to thee: "Why dost thou draw near to me, thou wretched being? Why dost thou desire me, thou miserable soul? I am not the good thing that thou seekest, seeing that thou desirest to love."

[1] Ps. iv. 9.

Look whither thou art going, go forward and do not quit the true and royal road that leads thee to thy God; while thou, although possessing all this, being still blind, foolish and infatuated, art not taking any heed to thyself, except to embrace that which doth not desire thee, that which continually drives thee out from itself, and thou succeedest under a storm of reproaches in detaining it against its will, and pursuest that which flies from thee and which, after all, is only given thee for mere service. And though thou desire it not, thou dost set it up in a kind of sovereignty over thee, so great is thy folly and vanity.

Moreover, those embraces will not last long for thee, for they will soon be converted into bitterness, and thou wilt very speedily be satiated, and will detest that which thou hast sought after with such eager desire, and such pains; and thou wilt forthwith seek after something else: and thus thou wilt go on in misery, no created thing being able to satisfy thee entirely,[1] as it is written, "the head of them compassing me about,"[2] and in another place he says, "The wicked walk round about".[3]

Wherefore return to God as to thy true centre; and let not the vanities of the world or the filth

---

[1] Literally, "to the circumference"; a phrase in correspondence with the allusions to the "centre" throughout this Meditation.

[2] Ps. cxxxix. 10; Vulg.   [3] *Ibid.*, xii. 9.

of the earth be the means of hindering thee. A large rock removed from its place and falling from a height is a frightful thing to behold, seeing with what impetus it descends, and with what a clatter it rushes downwards, and with what rapidity and velocity it hastens to reach the place which is suitable for it, and where it can be at rest; while all those things which put themselves in its way it crushes and breaks and destroys, in order that it may finally reach the place whither it is to go.

Thus, my soul, oughtest thou to give thyself to thy God and Creator, in order that thy shame and confusion may not be small when thou shalt see thyself outdone by a stone which runs to its centre with greater impetus than thou goest to thine. Lay aside, then, fling away [1] and destroy all that sets itself in thy way and obstructs thee from going to thy God. Break through it and pass on, as it is written, " and through my God I shall go over a wall ".[2]

Therefore, as thou art obstructed and hindered by some light wind of pride or envy, or by the impediment of a covetous desire for some worldly thing, whatever it may be, it is easy to understand of what little weight thou art and how like those light straws which, on account of their trifling weight, the wind arrests in its descent, and then whirls them in the air. But as for the rocks which

---

[1] "Derruecar," applied to a horse which throws its rider.
[2] Ps. xvii. 30.

fall, who can hold them? Who can stop them? In the same way, neither more nor less, the whole world can neither hinder the virtuous nor separate them from their God.

Behold S. Paul, an apostolical rock, and one of great weight, with what impetus he hastened towards his God, whom nothing could hinder from drawing near to his centre. "Who shall separate us," he says, "from the love of Christ? Shall tribulation, or distress, or famine, or nakedness, or danger, or persecution, or the sword? I am sure that neither death nor life, nor angels, nor principalities, nor powers, nor things present, nor things to come, nor might, nor height, nor depth, nor any other creature shall be able to separate us from the love of God which is in Jesus Christ our Lord."[1] O great, excellent, admirable weight of so holy a soul as that of this divine apostle! O most potent rock which by its weight and greatness destroyed and swept away all impediments in order that they might not hinder him from flying anywhere that he desired to go! Through distresses and through many troubles, through hunger and thirst, through heat and cold, through swords, through evil reports and through everything fearful and terrible, with the greatest alacrity he hastened onward towards his Centre, Whose will he had in some degree converted into a part of his own nature.

[1] Rom. viii. 35, 38, 39.

The rock by its natural impulse falls to its centre, but the soul does not do so, but by a voluntary and free impulse. This power, then, which God hath allowed thee, renounce, O my soul, and turn this liberty into nature, in order that thou mayst with all thy ability and all thy strength attain to the end whither thou art going. This is that which God commandeth thee, when He saith that thou must love Him with all thy heart, and with all thy soul, and with all thy mind, and with all thy power, and with all thy strength. Thou must understand that thou art to love Him according to the utmost of thy ability as thy natural instinct.

MEDITATION IX.

HOW LOVE LIFTS US UP TO GOD AS TO OUR CENTRE.

IT is a perfectly clear and well-authenticated truth, O Lord, that as Thou art the good of men, so all the power of love naturally inclines man to Thee, and carries him on to Thee as his beginning and centre; although he is often irregularly carried away to other things in opposition to his true worth and honour.

For just as our nature always directs us to one thing, so also does our whole will carry us towards one thing although owing to its uncontrolled choice it is capable of following after many, and at its pleasure it can turn whither it likes. For in the will there is no compulsion, as there is in nature, and would to God that there were, that we might even here be always united to Thee, as we shall, after this life, be united to Thee through Thy great mercy.

Alas! I see amongst men a great miracle, a very sad miracle, and one which is very greatly to be deplored. Wouldst thou not, peradventure, esteem it a great miracle if thou sawest a great rock suspended in the air, and that it had a wing? or if thou beheldest a river full of water, which, while running with great impetuosity, a mere piece of paper should be able to stop? Who that beheld such a sight would not bless[1] himself? Who would not wonder and be astounded? Why, then, am I not astonished at seeing men prevented by trivial things from attaining to Thee, my God? It is a very extraordinary thing that such trivialities as those of earth should keep back a man who naturally possesses within him a most momentous force which carries him towards Thee, my God.

We are pilgrims[2] in this world, and so the Divine Epistles call us, and we are travelling onward towards Thee, O Lord, as to our own country, and the native land of our souls, in which we live, as the apostle says,[3] and move and be. And whenever we sin we are hindered in the way, and halt there; and what is a great wonder and excites astonishment is that such trivial things should detain us.

My love is my weight,[4] and by my love I am carried whithersoever I wish to go. Wherever my love is inclined to rest, thither my soul goes; and as Thou, Lord, hast given weight to the rock in order that it may descend to its centre, which is its natural place, so Thou hast given to our

---

[1] Lit., "cross himself".   [2] Heb. xi. 13; 1 S. Peter ii. 11.
[3] Acts xvii. 28.   [4] *I.e.*, a force gravitating to its proper centre.

soul a weight which is the desire for the *summum bonum*, in order that by this weight it may be more easily drawn to Thee.

If this be so, then, O my good God, how can it be that every soul created for Thee doth not go with great haste unto Thee? But we see that, being lifted up and swept away by a little wind, it is deprived of all good, and is only laughed at, is spent and laid by as useless. How is it possible that any creature capable of enjoying Thee should not hasten with all its power towards Thee, its boundless, infinitely good, and consequently infinitely attractive centre? What thing can ever detain from such good a creature capable of enjoying it?

Oh how great is the weight of sin which, when laid upon the necks of human beings, presses them down and makes them sink to the ground, so that they do not mount up to their proper sphere, for which they were created. Truly this is a greater miracle that souls should not mount up to their God out of love for Him, than that rocks should be lifted up and swept off by a little wind, so that they should not descend to their centre: and still more wonderful than that a very thin sheet of paper should stop a rapid and full river from running onward to the sea.

Who would ever accept[1] his life with patience

---

[1] Endure the charge of.

if he knew clearly and distinctly how great a good he is deprived of, and what a benefit he is losing? O most graceless veil of my flesh, of how much joy dost thou deprive me? What hinders me from rending and tearing thee with my own hands that I may go and behold my God, and enjoy Him, and in Him find rest? Oh, of what pleasures and of what great happiness am I despoiled by thee, although, what is worse, knowing all this, and seeing it, and being well aware that it is so, I endure thee, and laugh at myself, and do not weep or groan (as would be more reasonable) day and night over such sad banishment and such blindness and miserable misfortune on my part!

Whence has such evil and graceless endurance come to me unless it is because this veil has been set in the midst and that cloud of the flesh so obstructs me that the brightness of the sun does not shine into the eyes of my soul? Take away this veil which impedes my sight, and thou shalt see with what powerful impetus my soul will rush towards its centre. Observe the souls of the saints, how light is their veil, and with what alacrity and swiftness they go to their God. Who can hinder them? Who can keep them back? Who can detach them from their proper place? *There* is full and perfect rest; *there* complete gratification for all the emotions and desires of the soul.

Truly the Lord is great and highly to be praised, and not the less to be loved, but as lovable as He is highly to be praised. When my soul shall be in the city of the Lord and in His holy mountain, the power of love shall be kindled, for no interposition of the fleshly veil shall obstruct it; and even now, when the veil is thin and transparent, the soul moves itself all the more towards its God, and the impulse of love is the more strengthened in it; while, on the contrary, in the case of those whose veil of flesh is gross there is little or no inclination towards the true centre of the soul. Such persons as these love God very little, or not at all. But those who by vigils and fastings, and other acts of abstinence, attenuate this fleshly veil and weaken its power, find this blessed light shining through the eyes of their souls, according to what the apostle says: "We see now through a glass in a dark manner".[1]

Such persons run after the odour of Thy ointments,[2] and even sometimes it happens to them that through some chinks and holes these rays of the Divine light shine at least for a short time into the eyes of their souls, and they immediately melt into love, and are lifted up with great impetus, not attracted by the odour, but by great beauty. But ah! how short a time this radiation of light endures, and how very quickly such delectable rays pass away! They strike the soul and immediately pass

---

[1] "Per speculum in enigmate," 1 Cor. xiii. 12 (Vulg.).

[2] "Post te curremus in odorem unguentorum tuorum," Cant. i. 3 (Vulg.).

away; and as Job says: "In His hands He hideth the light and commandeth it to come again. He showeth His friend concerning it, that it is His possession, and that he may come up to it."[1] But so soon as He kindles it between His hands, that which lies between His fingers flashes into light for a short time.

For if He chose to shine forth with all His light in full even at the doors of heaven, we must be aware that He would rather be likely to blind than to enlighten the heavenly spirits with His splendour, for they would be overcome by such exceeding brightness. For who could endure the Divine Majesty if it 'were not tempered? In this way spiritual men are entertained in this life until they see Thee, my God, clearly in the other world, where they will be perfectly in the centre of happiness, in the enjoyment of Thy Divine Essence.

[1] Job xxxvi. 32, 33.

MEDITATION X.

THAT THE SOUL IS AT REST ONLY IN GOD AS ITS CENTRE.

HOW naturally doth my soul lean towards Thee, my God, because of its love! Hence it is that if our nature were not deformed and depraved by sin, there would be no necessity that Thou shouldst *command* us to love Thee, just as now Thou hast not to command us to love ourselves, because being naturally disposed to give way to that affection even to excess, we have no need that Thou shouldst order and admonish us to do that which comes to us by nature and suits us.

Let us say at once, then, that there would be no necessity for such a command if nature were but preserved in that purity in which it was created; and hence it is that in its first creation we do not read that Thou didst give such a command either to the angels or to men when Thou didst create them; for they naturally inclined thereto, and those beings had no need of any stimulus to fulfil such an injunction who had been gloriously formed by their Creator according to an interior law of love.

But we have forgotten that natural law and we

are alienated from our own nature, insomuch that, neither for commands, nor promises, nor threatenings, nor daily and great benefits, do we ever love Thee as in all reason we ought. But just as a piece of lead which is detained by force on a high place if it be let go descends immediately to the ground, so our soul, if it be but for a little and forcibly carried away and lifted up to things of an exalted nature, immediately by its weight falls down to earthly and transitory things, and abandons itself entirely to those things of sense.

Tell me, then, O my soul, answer me, O miserable one, and declare to me what is the reason that thou pursuest the creature with such a keen appetite, so hungry and thirsty; and that so greatly to thy degradation thou goest begging of creatures a drop of muddy, tasteless and brackish water, which rather inflames thy thirst than quenches it, forsaking the pure, wholesome and perpetual fountain of all blessings, in which alone thou canst quench all thy thirst and gratify all thy pleasures and wishes.

Tell me, thou poor soul, what canst thou desire which thou wilt not find much more completely in thy God? If wisdom delights thee, He is most wise; if power and might, He is most powerful and mighty; if thou desirest glory and riches, He has abundance of both in His house; if delights and pleasures, "At Thy right hand are delights even to the end"; [1] if fulness and abundance of desire, those who possess Him are transported with the abundance of His house.

How, then, knowing this and much more than I could tell thee, O miserable, dost thou knowingly and of set purpose seek thy consolations and pleasures in the petty rills of the creature? Thou despisest the fountain which gives thee freely to drink, and with great labour dost dig for thyself turbid wells. O intolerable folly, flagrant extravagance and stupendous blindness! Hence it is that the Lord, being indignant at such conduct, exclaims by the mouth of the prophet, "Be astonished, O heavens, and let her gates be desolated, saith the Lord, for My people have done two evils. They have forsaken Me, the fountain of living water, and have digged to themselves cisterns, broken cisterns, that can hold no water." [2]

Truly the glory of the world is a dried-up and wasted cistern; the delight of the flesh is a dry well; and all honour and dignity is a ruined reservoir; all the abundance of riches is an open pool full of holes, which cannot hold water; and if thou believe me not, or thinkest that I am deceiving thee, then appeal to experience and observe that with whatever longing thou hast sought any dignity, and whatever troubles thou hast passed through in order to obtain it, when thou hast at-

---

[1] Ps. xv. 11; xxv. 8; cxi. 3.   [2] Jerem. ii. 13.

tained it, it seems to thee as nothing; for it is a pool full of holes and could not hold water. Thou hast longed for some delight, thou hast secured it, and immediately it disappears; for it is a cistern the contents of which have wasted away, and cannot retain the waters of delight that should be found there.

Very quickly do these vanities pass away and vanish like smoke, and, after all, thou hast got possession of a cistern as dry as before, and sometimes more dry and unsatisfying still. Experimentalise upon every kind of object, and thou wilt find that this is the case in all of them.

But although this be so, and unhappy men discover it by experience, with what trouble, under what affronts, with what drudgery do they dig out those wasted and broken wells in every direction! In order to excavate those putrid cisterns, they undergo great toils by day and night, by sea and land, in wars and in perils of death, and many of them in the laborious service of sin; while they make but little account of the pure fountain of living waters that flows through the market-places, nor do they set any value upon it though they are invited to partake thereof. This it is which cries out when calling to all people in the open places: "If any man thirst, let him come to Me and drink";[1]

[1] S. John vii. 37.

and in another place it cries by the mouth of a prophet,[1] saying: "All you that thirst, come to the waters; and you that have no money, make haste, buy and eat; come ye, buy wine and milk without money and without any price. Why do you spend money for that which is not bread, and your labour for that which doth not satisfy you?" Therefore it is that He complains to the angels and to His saints, saying: "Be astonished, O ye heavens";[2] ye must know, ye blessed angels, and wonder at this, ye who are set far apart from all woe and sorrow. But you, O ye gates, who are my saints that are still militant in the flesh, through whom as through gates many enter into heaven, afflict yourselves greatly and grieve much over such horrible and execrable blindness on the part of your people, over so great an error committed by wretched mortals, and over such great madness of the sons of Adam.

Quit, then, my soul, quit, I beseech thee, these exhausted, dried-up and broken cisterns which thou hast excavated with such toil, and with great haste run and betake thyself to the fountain which is thy God and Husband Jesus Christ, wherein thou mayst at thy pleasure quench all thy thirst. Here thou shalt be filled with delights, true delights and pleasures, after thy whole heart, thy whole will, and as thou desirest. Only in the Lord wilt thou find

---

[1] Isa. lv. 1.   [2] Jerem. ii. 12.

peace and rest, and in no other thing whatsoever of all that is in the world. He only is thy centre, thy proper and natural sphere; out of Him shalt thou find no contentment, but in Him all good, rest and glory.

MEDITATION XI.

THAT WE OUGHT TO LOVE GOD BECAUSE HE LOVES US.

IF so many reasons as there are for loving Thee, O God of my heart and Spouse of my soul, do not suffice to make my heart burn day and night with the flame of devotion to Thee, at least the boundless love which Thou bearest towards me ought to awaken me and move me a little. Nothing is more provocative of love than the being loved; and thus it is that we love those who love us, although they may be unworthy of our affection, solely because they love us.

Who is so heathenish and barbarous as not to love one who loves him? The most hard-hearted men are wont to love those who love them. Yet they do not desire to act thus towards Thee, even being what Thou art, and though loving them so much that Thou hast given Thyself for them. Since one love is not satisfied except with another love, it is certainly very just, O Lord, that I should love Thee, and that I should burn with a living flame of the pure fire of love, since I am so fervently loved by Thee.

If, my soul, thou doubtest the love which God

bears to thee, consider the witnesses to His love. The cross is a witness, the nails are witnesses, the pains, the tumult, the streams of blood are witnesses, and the bitter and cruel death which He suffered for thee is a witness. He endured all this, and it appeared to Him but little in proportion to the greatness of His love; and if it were possible, He would even entreat and desire to endure greater things for thee, greater sorrows, greater anguish, and greater pains, for this is what He meant by His cry upon the cross, when He said that He thirsted. And although it is written of Him that He shall be full of troubles,[1] and the Scripture in another place saith also that His soul shall be filled with evils,[2] yet with all this He desires to be filled to the utmost,[3] and He thirsts with insatiable longing.[4]

Truly He endured enough, for from the sole of His foot to His head He had no soundness, and yet He thirsted for more. If, then, my soul, thou art cold in loving a Being of so great love, thou showest thyself harder than the rocks, since thou knowest that before such condescension they broke asunder,[5] hard as they were, and those things which had no feeling still showed feeling. If the very rocks could not endure so great a weight of love, learn from the hardest rocks to love thy Creator.

[1] Lament. iii. 61.   [2] Ps. lxxxvii. 4.   [3] "Cuanto al efecto."
[4] "Cuanto al afecto."   [5] S. Matt. xxvii. 51.

Why, then, dost thou not soften thyself, O miserable, seeing that the rocks were rent asunder at such great favour, and that those rocks performed the office of hearts for men? Become, then, a disciple of the rocks, and learn to love. The most precious gift that Thou hast given us, O our God, and the greatest that we have received from Thy Divine hands, was love. Thy love towards men was a gift, and an interior favour, hidden, secret, intimate, and the source and foundation of all other gifts and favours. For just as one concludes that there must be fire where we see smoke and sparks coming forth, so we conclude with respect to the love which Thou bestowest upon us through the good things which Thou hast done in us and for us. In this way Thou commendest Thyself by the prophet Malachi, saying: "I have loved you, saith the Lord".[1]

Thou drawest forth the love of Thyself, not by change, but by communication. Thou hast created the heavens and filled them with angels; Thou hast created the air and filled it with birds, the sea with fishes, and the earth with animals; but for man Thou hast provided a habitation in Thyself. Thus Thou saidst to the patriarch Abraham: "I am thy reward exceeding great".[2] The love which Thou bearest to man is shown in the favours which Thou bestowest on him. Thou lovest us so much, O Lord, that even in those chastisements which Thou layest upon us,

[1] Mal. i. 2. [2] Gen. xv. 1.

Thou endeavourest to promote our good and profit, and desirest that we should know, humble, and amend ourselves.

When Thou didst send those seven plagues upon Egypt Thou saidst to Moses: "And the Egyptians shall know that I am the Lord".[1] Thou didst desire to make Thyself known to these Gentiles, in order that, abandoning their idolatry, they might serve Thee and might themselves be saved. In the Gospel Thou commandest that the servant should be sold who owed ten thousand talents, in order that being amended by his chastisement he might humble himself, and might be found worthy of having all his debt forgiven.

O how good Thou art towards us, Thou God of Israel, and how greatly dost Thou love us, since equally in prosperity as in the tribulations which Thou sendest to us, Thou seekest our profit; and thus, O Lord, Thou lovest not only that in me which cometh from Thyself, but also even that which is peculiarly my own, and which comes from my free will, if it be good, while Thou abhorrest the evil that is in me. Wherefore if it were possible to chastise the sin of those who are in hell without chastising their persons, Thou wouldst do so, because Thou lovest our human nature so much. But since it is not possible to chastise the one without the other, because the faults and sins are accidents and

[1] Exod. vii. 5.

cannot exist without a substance, for this reason when Thou punishest the one Thou punishest the other.

If a wound be inflicted on any one, and after it has been healed the mark still remains, although he abhors the wound and the mark, he loves the flesh where the injury was inflicted. Even so, Lord, Thou lovest the creatures whom Thou hast made, while abhorring the sins and faults which proceed from the human will. In the book of Wisdom it is written that Thou hatest none of the things that Thou hast made:[1] "For God made not death, neither hath He pleasure in the destruction of the living".[2] But the wickedness of the perverse will is the author of sin; wherefore by punishing in hell the evil that man has done, Thou preservest his nature, which is a good gift of Thine; for Thy love continues unchangeable in its affection for that nature which Thou hast created; and thus in all that Thou doest for us, O Lord, Thou showest the great love that Thou entertainest for us, and all the benefits which Thou dost confer upon men proceed from that burning and most ardent love wherewith Thou lovest us.

Predestination springs from love; the creation of the heaven and the earth and of all other things is the fruit of love. Wherefore as Thou, Lord, desirest that we should imitate Thee in

---

[1] Wisd. xi. 25.

[2] *Ibid.*, i. 13. The Vulg. reads: "Nec lætatur in perditione vivorum," which exactly accords with the Greek.

all things, so Thou desirest that all our actions should come forth enkindled with charity; and hence it comes to pass that Thou art not willing to accept anything that does not present itself adorned with charity: and the reason is that he who giveth Thee gold or silver is bestowing on Thee outward things merely; but he who loves Thee giveth himself to Thee; and this is the cause why Thou dost so liberally reward the services which we render Thee; because Thou dost find in them the love that we owe Thee.

Thou sayest, Lord, in Thy Gospel, that as the Father hath loved Thee, so Thou hast loved us,[1] for as the Father loved Thee in that human nature which Thou didst take upon Thee out of Thy graciousness, so Thou lovest us out of Thy kindness without any merits of our own. How is it, then, my soul, that thou wilt not love Him Who loveth thee so deeply? So soon as thou beginnest to love thy God, thou wilt find such joy and delight in that love, that thou wilt experience greater misery in relinquishing it, lest thou lose such great sweetness, than the trouble which will fall to thy lot in really breaking with the world for the love of thy Spouse Jesus Christ. This doth not bring torment to any one, since it is a greater sorrow to forsake the love of God after thou hast tasted it, than to break with the world and to begin to love thy God.

[1] S. John xv. 9.

MEDITATION XII.

THAT WE OUGHT TO LOVE GOD BECAUSE HE FIRST LOVED US.

IN desiring that we should love Thee, O Lord, Thou hast thought good to love us first; in order that by thus alluring us, we being thus forestalled by Thy grace, might not be able to fail in loving Thee. Thou hast found no better means than to love first those by whom Thou seekest to be loved. Thou hast first loved us, saith S. John.[1] For putting aside that Thy love is infinite and cannot be repaid, the fact of having first loved us is a favour so paramount that it is impossible for us to requite it.

David could never repay to Jonathan that first love with which Jonathan loved David, and that generosity which he displayed in giving him his own robes in token of the great affection which he entertained for him.[2] Wherefore David, feeling himself under such an obligation to repay the love which he owed to Jonathan, loved him as his own life, and not only loved him while living,

---

[1] 1 S. John iv. 19. [2] 1 Kings xviii. 3, 4.

but also exhibited the great attachment which he felt towards him on the occasion of his death,[1] when he wept over him with such profound grief.

I must love Thee, then, my God, my refuge and my strength,[2] for Thy great mercies. Although Thou art wonderful in all Thy works, yet in the disposition of mercy which Thou showest towards man I find Thee more wondrous still. "Thy tender mercies," saith the prophet, "are over all Thy works."[3] Thou refusest no one, Thou castest away none, Thou despisest none, and those who offend Thee and fly from Thee Thou still seekest with perseverance, and callest upon graciously. Thou pardonest him that repenteth; Thou receivest him that returneth, and hopest for him that delayeth his repentance. Thou turnest the wanderer back again into the right way; invitest him that refuseth Thee, awakest the careless, embracest him that cometh to Thee, consolest the sorrowful, liftest up the fallen, and openest to him that crieth to Thee.

It is a strange thing that the sinner who forsakes Thee, Thou *Summum Bonum* and infinite Goodness, not finding any rest in the things which he loves, does not seek a remedy by returning to Him Whom he has offended. He cannot live without Thee, and by separating himself from Thee, he is necessarily compelled to return to

---

[1] 2 Kings i. 17.   [2] Ps. xvii. 2, 3.
[3] *Ibid.*, cxliv. 9.

Thee. The prodigal son, not finding anything but troubles and miseries in all created things, had no other remedy than that of returning to his father whom he had disregarded.[1] Thou art our protection and shelter, and Thou hast so loved us that in order to gain our love Thou hast (as Isaias saith) borne our infirmities and carried our sorrows.[2] Thou hast bartered with us Thy good things for our evil ones; Thou weepest that we may laugh, and fastest that we may eat; Thou toilest for our rest, art poor in order to enrich us, and finally dost die that we might live. We have laid infirmity upon Thee, and Thou hast bestowed health on us. "For you know the grace of our Lord Jesus Christ, that being rich He became poor for your sakes; that through His poverty you might be rich."[3]

However much husband and wife or brother and sister may love each other, they will always be distinct personalities. But the infinite love which Thou bearest to us has effected this, that Thy Divine Nature and our humanity should be united in a single Person. Solomon says that "he who is a friend loveth at all times, and a brother is proved in distress".[4] O true Friend of my soul, Who hast loved me at all times! in honour and dishonour, in life and in death; and since Thou hadst no other liberty than that of speech wherewith to do

---

[1] S. Luke 15.   [2] Isa. liii. 4.
[3] 2 Cor. viii. 9.   [4] Prov. xvii. 17.

us a favour when Thou wast nailed upon the Cross, with that Thou didst gain for me the pardon of the Father, praying with tears, as Thy holy apostle saith.[1]

When we were least worthy of being loved, then didst Thou all the more declare the love which Thou bearest towards us, displaying it in greater works. Thou didst preach more often and perform more miracles in Capharnaum than in other cities of the Kingdom of Judæa or of the province of Galilee, in order that in that maritime city where there were more sins and vices, and the inhabitants were less worthy of Thy presence, Thy mercy should shine forth more brightly, according to that which Thy holy apostle said, "Where sin abounded grace did more abound".[2]

Who would not love so loving a God, Who does not disdain to love even where He is but little loved? Who could have a heart so horrible and full of sin as to despair of the mercy of God, seeing that He did not turn away His face from the idolatries, avarice, and infamy of Capharnaum? I know not who could have a breast so hardened or a heart so frozen, as not to be softened and melted by the presence of so great a love. S. Luke the evangelist in describing how, on the night of Thy Sacred Passion, Thou didst withdraw Thyself from Thy disciples about a stone's throw in order to pray

---

[1] Heb. v. 7.   [2] Rom. v. 20.

in the garden, uses the word *avulsus*.[1] This word *avulsus* is properly to root up, as when one puts forth great force in uprooting a tree with its root and the earth around it. Thy heart was so united in love to those apostles that Thou didst separate Thyself from them as if Thy bowels were being extirpated.

O great strength of love which even for so short a distance as a stone's throw could not endure absence without great pain, whereas thou, my soul, art separated from thy God so many years and art scarcely sensible of it! Thou art wanting in the love of God; thou canst not deny it. This great love did not suffer Him to detach Himself half a league from His own creatures, nay, not even so short a space as a stone's throw.

God is love, He is tender and most sweet: wherefore there is no greater delight than holy love. God is love, and is not faith, but the basis and object upon which our faith is founded. S. John says only that God is love; whence we may understand how natural it is for Him to love us, since we are the work of His Hands. Oh with what justice does He desire to be loved with all our

---

[1] S. Luke xxii. 41 (Vulg.). There is no support in the original Greek for this version, or for the comment which the author of these Meditations builds upon the term employed in the Latin Vulgate. The Greek simply means "drew away from"; the same verb being used in S. Matt. xxvi. 51, to describe the drawing out of a sword from its sheath. The Rheims translation, "was withdrawn away from them," is perfectly correct.

WE OUGHT TO LOVE GOD WHO FIRST LOVED US. 69

strength and heart, seeking the homage of our soul alone, since to Him only is our entire choice and love due! O sweetness of holy love; and how well did the name—given to Thee by the special friend of God—suit Thee, when he said: "God is charity, and he that abideth in charity abideth in God and God in him".[1] O admirable companionship and barter of great gain, that being such as I am, Thou, my God, givest Thyself in exchange with me, and that as I love Thee Thou lovest me, to repay love with love.

Love is free, for it springs from a free source, which is our will. For this reason love is so precious and Thou cravest it in us, O Lord, as our jealous friend; for it is the richest jewel of our own that we can offer Thee. For that precious pearl and flaming ruby of love Thou hast given to man the whole creation, having made him lord of this universe, as saith the psalmist;[2] whence in giving him all, Thou hast bound him to repay this with all the debt of love which he owes to Thee as to his Creator.

Thou didst place man first in the gardens of the earthly Paradise;[3] Thou madest him lord of the universe, and didst prepare[4] him with singular gifts and many blessings in order that he might love Thee. But since much wood usually extinguishes the fire, and ends in producing smoke only, so Adam

---

[1] 1 S. John iv. 16.   [2] Ps. viii. 6.   [3] Gen. ii. 15.
[4] "Prevent" him, Ps. xx. 4.

loaded with so many favours went forth[1] weeping, when, owing to his ingratitude, the Divine fire of love died out of his miserable heart. But Thou, my Lord and my Redeemer, like the Cherubim desiring to feed fire with fire, didst enter beneath the wheels of my afflictions, and taking live coals in Thy Sacred Hands, didst spread them over the city of Jerusalem, which is every one of our souls, according to what the prophet Ezechiel beheld in a vision.[2]

[1] Gen. iii. 24.   [2] Ezech. x. 2, 6, 7.

MEDITATION XIII.

THAT THE LOVE WHICH GOD BEARS TO US IS ETERNAL AND COEVAL WITH HIMSELF.

THE great love which Thou, O Lord, bearest towards us in loving us manifested itself before Thou wast loved by us. Thy love was not the requital of my love, neither could my love satisfy that affection which Thou didst entertain for me. In loving me first consists the proof of love, and Thou hast first loved me from eternity, according to that saying of the prophet,[1] "His mercy endureth for ever, and His truth to generation and generation".

The holy king employed the term "mercy" in speaking of Thy sacred love because this appellative of mercy gives me a more complete knowledge of what Thou art than the name of love. Mercy is an affection of the mind which commiserates another's sorrow and provides for the person who is in necessity, first bestowing upon him the compassion of the soul. Setting aside that which is out of character with Thy Nature as an impassible Being, I will consider that which properly belongs to Thee as an attribute, and will remark upon love.

[1] Ps. xcix. 5.

Compassion and a sorrowful heart do not pertain to Thee, because Thy nature is the essence of perfection and glory; but it does peculiarly belong to Thee to provide for the poor and needy. I know the blessings which Thou hast bestowed upon me in loving me, and this in the name of mercy; for Thou hast found in me no beauty or good things to attract Thy love, but misery for Thee to heal and poverty to enrich.

For this reason the prophet employs the name of mercy rather than that of love: and thus hast Thou loved me, a miserable sinner, without any merits of mine, solely because of Thy goodness and love; and this love so surely existed before I came into being that S. John in saying that Thou didst first love us, and David in singing that Thy mercy is everlasting, both declare the endlessness of Thy love, because Thou hast loved us without beginning and eternally.

Thou knowest all things in Thyself, and it is not necessary that they should be actually done or that they should play a good or an evil part in order to be made fully known to Thee; for since Thou dost not receive knowledge from created things, so Thou hast no occasion to wait for what men do in order to understand their works. There can be no novelty nor accident in Thy case, for that would be a great imperfection, while the least imperfection must be very far from Thee. Wherefore, when I perceive

Thee doing anything new, I do not conceive that Thou art then possessed by a new will nor that Thou art then desiring something for the first time; but my thoughts revert to that most remote and eternal disposition of Thine whereby Thou hast eternally ordained all things and determined everything that we see done anew.

The things are new to our eyes, are eternal to Thine, since before they are done Thou knowest them; and thus Thy mercy and love are eternal, because in Thy eternity Thou beholdest and knowest perfectly the misery of our sin, and whereas we are worthy of condemnation, Thou hast shown mercy by having compassion upon us, and hast effectively sought to give us in due time grace and glory in order to heal our wounds and overcome death, bestowing upon us the resurrection and life.

Consider now, therefore, O my soul, how strongly thou art bound to the Divine love because of thy God having loved thee so greatly before thou couldst have any good desires towards Him. Measure that couple of hours which have passed since thou didst begin to exist with the eternity of God during which He loved thee. A thousand years are in the Divine esteem but as yesterday which quickly passes away.[1] Compare one with the other, and thou wilt find thyself abashed and overcome; and would to God that thou wouldst comply with the law of those who are

[1] Ps. lxxxix. 4.

conquered and placed in subjection to the power of the Conqueror! Would to God that thou couldst find thyself so bound and overcome as to remain a captive to the love of Him Who so loved thee in His eternity, in order that thou mightest be free from those chains of fire in which all the sinners of the earth will be imprisoned!

Never, O Lord, hast Thou repented of having done good to us however ungrateful Thou hast known us to be, nor hast Thou turned back in Thy mercies; for, as the apostle saith, "The gifts and calling of God are without repentance".[1] In Thee there is neither yea nor nay, for Thou remainest so faithful and true for ever. I began to exist yesterday, and have wasted my days idly, and what is worse, in a thousand offences against Thee. Many times I have resolved to love Thee and I have turned back, and when I have begun sometimes to serve Thee I have turned to offend Thee. Of this my heart is witness, and so are the angels and every creature.

Oh, what great dishonour and shame! Oh, confusion full of safety if I could only know it! Peradventure Thou didst wait until the time should arrive in which Thou shouldst come in the flesh[2] in order to seek my good? Perhaps the deformity of my offence hindered Thy Divine goodness and beauty from cherishing me? O my God, infinite

---

[1] Rom. xi. 29.   [2] "Tiempo en que nacieses."

goodness, eternal love and true salvation! I knew Thee not, not even for many years after I came into existence; and when at length out of Thy boundless charity Thou hadst given me the grace to know Thee, and Thy great beauty and goodness had affected me, I fixed my love on the foulness and corruption of the creature, forsaking Thy love Who art infinite goodness and glory, and the beauty of the angels. I remained in the love of the creatures, when Thy Paternal care had bestowed them on me for my refreshment and service, for the manifestation of which goodness Thou art worthy of all love and reverence.

Thy goodness, O Lord, and my wickedness contended against each other; and the more kind and generous Thou didst show Thyself towards me, so much the more rebellious didst Thou find me, and ungrateful for the blessings which I received from Thy bounty. My ingratitude did not exhaust the fountain of Thy mercy, for Thy goodness and clemency overcome all human wickedness; and just as love does not know how to be idle, but manifests itself in deeds, so for the love Thou bearest us Thou hast given us gifts of nature and grace, and hast promised us gifts of glory if we keep Thy commandments.

Why, then, O my God, and infinite goodness, will my heart not love Thee, when I see that I am forestalled by Thy love and that Thou hast been beforehand in seeking and loving me and hast shown the sovereign love which Thou bearest me by so many benefits? The first things that my eyes beheld when I was born were the gifts of Thy Hand with which Thou didst take possession of my heart that I might love Thee perpetually.

As the *primum mobile* carries along with it the other spheres and the heavens, moving them from east to west, so the force of that Holy love which Thou hadst for me from the first in Thy eternity carries away with it all the powers of the soul and the senses of the body, subjecting them to the sweet service of the yoke of Thy holy love. This is what the Bride in the Song of Songs asks of Thee as a peculiar favour: "Draw me; we will run after Thee in the odour of Thy ointments".[1] From the knowledge of these things it follows that I find myself under a strong obligation to love Him Who, loving me of old and eternally, has bound me with such great benefits.

[1] Cant. i. 3.

MEDITATION XIV.

WHENCE IT IS THAT THE LOVE WHICH CHRIST BEARETH TO US HAS ITS SOURCE.

IF, after contemplating the eternity of the love wherewith Thou didst forestall me, I desire to consider the greatness of that love, in such a meditation, O my Redeemer and Lord, all created intelligence would be exhausted. There is no tongue that would be competent to express it; and Thy apostle S. Paul saith that Thy charity surpasseth all knowledge[1] and sense, even though it be that of the angels. What man, then, can expound it if the angels cannot compass the knowledge thereof?

Some, erroneously reasoning, have thought it impossible that Thou shouldst love us. For since all love springs from the goodness and perfection of the thing which is loved, and since the food of love is the goodness and perfectness of things, man being a creature so low and so imperfect in his body, and in his soul a mere vessel of iniquity, what love can attach itself to a creature so wretched?

If, moreover, they take into especial consideration that Thy Divine Love is neither blind nor impassioned

[1] Ephes. iii. 19.

nor capricious, they would believe erroneously that the love which Thou entertainest for us is trifling if they think that it has its source in ourselves. For where there is neither blindness nor passion in the person who loves and the thing which he loves is so imperfect, deformed and wretched, the love must be but slight. But Thy Holy Love, O Lord, does not spring from any perfection that exists in us, but from that which Thou ever beholdest in Thy Eternal Father.

The fulness of perfection and the riches of grace which were bestowed by the Holy Trinity on the most sacred Manhood of our Redeemer were conferred on Him at the moment of His conception. At that moment were bestowed on Him three graces so great that each one of them is in its own way infinite, *viz.*, the grace of the Divine Union; the universal grace which was given to Him as the Head of the whole Church; and the essential grace of His Soul.

He first united this Holy Manhood with the Divine Personality in such sort that we can with truth affirm that this Man is God, and the Son of God, and that He is to be worshipped as God both in heaven and on earth. This grace is clearly infinite, because of the gift which is bestowed in it, which is the greatest that can be conferred, since in it God gives Himself; as well as in respect to the mode in which this boon is administered, which is the most intimate that exists, *viz.*, by means of personal union; and thus Christ is not two persons, but one person, and an infinite substance.

He [God] also bestowed on this New Man that He should be the universal father and first principle of all men, in order that as their spiritual Head He might infuse into them His own virtue; so that so far as He is God, He is equal to the Eternal Father, while in so far as He is Man He is the Beginning and Head of all men; and in conformity with this pre-eminence He [God] conferred upon Him infinite grace, in order that from Him as from a fountain of grace and a sea of holiness all men might receive grace; and He is entitled Holy of Holies, not only because He is greater than all, but because of His being the Sanctifier of all, and, if one may say so, a *dye* of holiness from which every one who is to be sanctified may receive that colour and lustre [which represents sanctification by His precious blood]. This grace also is in a sense infinite, because it is for the whole race, so that the number of persons is not in any way limited, but so far as He is concerned it may be multiplied infinitely, while for every one included therein the merits and grace are multiplied in the blessed soul of Jesus Christ.

God particularly bestowed another special grace upon Him, in order to the sanctification and perfection of His life, which may also be entitled infinite, because He possesses all that pertains to grace in the most perfect conceivable degree.

Moreover, in the moment of His most holy conception there were conferred upon Him all graces freely given for the working of miracles and wonders, as many as He would.[1] These were all conferred upon Him in the highest measure and perfection; for this is that fair flower of beauty on which the white dove of the Holy Spirit rested, and extending its wings, covered Him, and spread over Him all its virtues and graces. This is the chosen vessel from which is most abundantly poured that bounteous river of all graces with all its streams, without a single drop failing to enter it. Herein God bestowed the greatest benefit He had to give, and conferred all that could be so given; for herein He exercised the extreme of power and grace, in lavishing all that He could on that most blessed soul at the very moment when it became a creature.

And above all, there was given to it at the same moment to behold immediately the Divine Essence and to recognise clearly the majesty and glory of the Word with which it was united, and thus beholding to be blessed and filled with the same essential glory as it now enjoys at the right hand of the Father. If so great a gift excites your admiration, there is another wonderful circumstance connected with it, which is that He [God] gave all this out of pure free grace

[1] Isa. lxi. 1.; S. Luke iv. 18.

independently of all merit and before this blessed soul could have performed any meritorious act whatever whereby it could have deserved such bounty.

The creation of that soul and the bestowal of all these graces upon it were accomplished only because the Lord was desirous in this way to enlarge and spread out His hands and bounty and thus to magnify His grace, on which account S. Augustine calls Christ the exemplar and model of grace. For just as great writers and painters are wont to make some patterns or models of the works of their craft when they wish to make them known, wherein employing all their knowledge they exert their ability to the utmost in order that the whole world may see how important is the object at which they are aiming; so the goodness and greatness of God resolved to create a new creature, and to exercise upon it, in His own fashion, all His greatness and grace in order that by that work the greatness of God might be known in heaven and on earth.

King Assuerus made a most solemn feast in order that all his kingdoms might behold the greatness of his riches and power.[1] The King of heaven desired to make another most wonderful feast for that Holy Humanity whereto He was betrothed, in order that all creatures both in heaven and earth should know thereby the greatness of the Divine goodness and bounty which extended itself to such matters.

[1] Esth. i. 1-4.

Behold then, now, my soul, what an admirable gift this is, and how happy was that blessed soul of thy Redeemer on which God was pleased to bestow such grace; do not entertain envy, but joy, since the grace which He received He partook of not solely on His own account, but also for thee. In His Name are these words of Job written: "If I have eaten my morsel alone, and the fatherless hath not eaten thereof (for from my infancy mercy grew up with me, and it came out with me from my mother's womb)".[1] Thus He did not eat His morsel alone, but rather divided it with strangers, and our true Head received what He obtained not for Himself alone, but for His members as well.

[1] Job xxxi. 17, 18.

MEDITATION XV.

OF THE ORIGIN AND CAUSE OF THE LOVE OF JESUS CHRIST.

RECALL now, therefore, thy thoughts, O my soul; enter into thyself, and in silence and solitude pause awhile, and consider the portion of such great riches as these which belong to thee. Tell me, when that most holy soul of Jesus Christ in that happy moment when it was created, opened its eyes and perceived itself to be such as it appeared, and knew so well from Whose hands it had come, and that it was born a king, and found itself at the head of all creation, and beheld all the hierarchies of heaven in the attitudes of adoration before it who at that moment worshipped Him as the apostle says;[1] tell me, if it can possibly be expressed, with what love such a soul would love that which thus sought to glorify it? With what longing would it desire to offer all in its power to please and serve such a giver? Is there any language of the Cherubim or Seraphim which could express it?

Then I must add further; it was in respect to this desire that it was said that the Will of God was

[1] Heb. i. 6.

to seek and to save the human race which had been lost by the offence of one man, and that He burdened Himself with this office out of His reverence and obedience; and that He took to heart this glorious design and never rested until He had gone through with it. As then the Son of God when invested with humanity took upon Himself this work of redeeming men, He must needs love them with such affection and desire that, out of His longing to see them healed and restored to their primeval glory, He might be able to do and to suffer all that was necessary to that end.

After this generous soul knew of this necessity, being desirous to please the Eternal Father with an offspring of ineffable love, He endeavoured by His love and tenderness towards them to bring back men through this obedience to the Father. We see that when any piece of ordnance discharges a shot with much powder and force, if the ball rebounds obliquely from the point at which it was aimed, it rebounds with so much greater impetus in proportion to the greater force with which it was impelled. Just so this love of the soul of Jesus Christ towards God carried such admirable force because the powder of that grace which impelled it was infinite, that after it had gone straight and pierced the heart of the Father, there rebounded from thence the love of men; and there is neither language nor power to express with what force and gladness it returned upon them to love them and heal them. This is that force which the prophet indicates when he says: "He hath rejoiced as a giant to run the way; His going out is from the end of heaven and His circuit even to the end thereof, and there is no one that can hide himself from His heat".[1]

O Love Divine that camest forth from God, and didst descend to man, and didst return to God, because Thou didst not love man for man's sake but for God, and Thou didst love him in such sort that whosoever reflects upon this love cannot resist Thy love, for it possesses power over all hearts, as Thy holy apostle saith: "For the charity of Christ presseth us".[2] This is that fervour and devotion which Thy holy Church depicts in the Song of Songs when she says: "Behold He cometh leaping upon the mountains, skipping over the hills. My beloved is like a roe, or a young hart".[3] The prophet Isaias signifies the same thing when he says: "He shall not fail nor be discouraged until He has established judgment and order in the earth, and the isles shall hope in Him".[4] From hence spring those exalted words which Thou hast uttered: "I will not give sleep to mine eyes, and scarcely let mine eyelids close, nor take any rest for my life until I find out on earth a dwelling-place and habitation amongst men".[5]

This is the source and origin of the love of Christ

---

[1] Ps. xviii. 6, 7.   [2] 2 Cor. v. 14.   [3] Cant. ii. 8, 9.
[4] Isa. xlii. 4.   [5] Paraphrase of Ps. cxxxi. 4, 5.

for men, if thou desire to know; for neither the virtue, the goodness, nor the beauty of man was the cause of this love; but the virtues of Christ, His favour and His grace, and His ineffable affection towards God. Such is the meaning of His words when He said to His disciples on the Thursday of the Supper: "That the world may know how much I love My Father, let us arise and go hence to the place where I must die upon the cross for men".[1]

See now, therefore, my soul, the cause of so great a love as this. The splendour of the sun burns so much the more as his rays are more strongly refracted. The rays of fire from this Divine Sun went straight to the heart of God, and from thence were refracted upon men. If then those rays are so direct, how must His splendour burn? No angelic intellect can comprehend how this fire doth glow, nor how far its efficacy reaches. Thou desirest, Lord, that we should repay this love of Thine with our love, and that we should love Thee in return for that boundless love wherewith Thou hast loved and dost love us. The love which Thou hadst and still hast for us, placed Thee on the cross; and in order to be loved by us Thou didst deliver Thyself unto death.

O my good Jesus! how well I now understand that which Thou saidst: "I am come to cast fire on the earth, and what will I but that it be kindled?"[2] I see Thee entirely consumed by love, and with

---

[1] Paraphrase of S. John xiv. 31.   [2] S. Luke xii. 49.

thousands of tongues of fire, and with wounds almost innumerable. Thou dost encounter my soul which is hemmed in on all sides by a fire of pitch which is Thy most holy love. I know not how it is that it has not already submitted, yielding itself freely into the hands of Thy Divine Majesty, since it cannot be that any one would die who would freely surrender himself into the hands of Him Who is the true Life according to that which Thou saidst to holy Martha: " I am the resurrection and the life ".[1]

What dost thou fear, my soul? Why dost thou resist Him Who is of infinite power? A Seraph is inflamed with love; fear not, but love Him Who demands love only. If thou fly from life, what remains but thou must find death? and if thou fear death, why dost thou not give thyself up when Jesus Christ is offering thee life, in Whom, as His apostle saith, thou hast life, being and movement?[2] Behold how greatly thy Spouse Jesus Christ loves thee, and do not either stop or take rest until thou art altogether converted to His love, and become a living coal inflamed with the pure fire of love, as thou art bound to desire Him Who loves thee after so wondrous a manner.

[1] S. John xi. 25.   [2] Acts xvii. 28.

MEDITATION XVI.

THAT THIS LOVE OF CHRIST IS WITHOUT LIMIT.

THE love that Thou bearest to us is of such a nature, O our Lord and Redeemer, and the Life of my soul, and it is so profound, that the limit of Thy love is not that it lasts until death whenever it comes, even the death of the cross, but extends much further; for if as Thou didst receive commandment to suffer one death, they should command Thee to undergo thousands of deaths, Thou wouldst cherish love for them all; and if that which they commanded Thee to suffer for all men, they should command Thee to perform for each one of them, Thou wouldst have done this for each one as for all; and if, as Thou wast hanging on the cross for those three hours, it had been necessary for Thee to remain there until the day of judgment, Love would have sufficed for that. So that Thou, O Lord, hast loved much more than Thou hast suffered, and a much greater love possessed Thee enclosed in Thy heart than that which Thou didst show forth externally in Thy wounds. It was not without a great mystery that the Holy Spirit desired it to be written amongst the other particulars of the temple of Solomon, *viz.*, that the windows of the temple were wider and more open on the inside than on the outside, and thus they were larger inside than they appeared without.[1] O Divine Love! how much more loving wert Thou in Thy inner being than Thou didst appear externally! So many wounds, so many scourgings, and such cruel outrages, doubtless do preach to us of the greatest love, but they do not tell us *all* the greatness of that love, for without doubt that love was much greater which burned within Thy sacred bosom than that which appeared externally. Those wounds were the sparks which issued from that fire; they were a branch that grew out of that tree; a rivulet that flowed from this infinite sea of boundless love. This is the sign that love has to show, *viz.*, to lay down its life for its friends; a sign or mark, but not an exact equality. If then I owe Thee so much, my God and my Lord, for that which Thou hast done for me, how much more must I owe Thee for that Thou hast desired to do! If that was so great a boon which was public and which the eyes of all beheld, how much greater is that which only the eyes of God behold! O sea of infinite love, O boundless depth of affection! who could doubt, O Lord, the love which Thou hast towards us? Who would not esteem himself the richest being in the world since he is beloved by

[1] 3 Kings vi. 4; compare Ezech. xl. 16, and xli. 16.

such a Lord? I beseech Thee, my Saviour, by those bowels of mercy which moved Thee to bestow upon me such a gift, that Thou wouldst give me eyes and a heart that I may know and feel this, and may always glory in Thy mercies, and sing Thy praises all the days of my life. If then, my soul, thou desirest to discover something of the greatness of thy Lord's love, and of the longing which He felt to suffer for thee, set thyself to meditate on the greatness of the desire which the saints felt to suffer for God, and thereby thou wilt be able to understand something of the longing which the Holiest of the holy ones felt, since it exceeded all others in holiness and grace as much as the light of the sun overpowers the darkness, and much more. Consider the desire which those blessed fathers, S. Francis and S. Dominic, felt, who wished for martyrdom as the hart desireth the water-brooks, while the glorious S. Dominic prayed that all the members of his body might be mutilated, considering that martyrdom alone was but a small matter, and desiring a martyrdom for every member. Consider, too, the wish of the blessed apostle S. Andrew, who, when he saw the cross on which he had to suffer, embraced it as a beloved spouse, and asked if it rejoiced with him as he was satisfied with it. I come to another much more exalted martyrdom, and a new kind of desire, *viz.*, that of S. Paul, who, considering that all kinds of suffering joined together were but a small thing to satisfy the love which he felt towards God, desired the very pains and torments of hell itself, for the honour of God and the salvation of men. "I wished myself," says the holy apostle, "to be an anathema from Christ for my brethren."[1] He therein desired to be for ever separated from Christ so far as regards any participation in His glory, though not in respect to the grace and love of God. Take then now, my soul, wings to fly and mount this step towards the bowels and heart of thy Spouse Jesus Christ, and consider that if this holy apostle having only one drop of grace was possessed of such love to men, how much greater must be the longings of the Saviour Who is a boundless sea of grace, for in proportion to the love is the longing. This, O Lord, is what Thou desirest us to understand in those words of Thine when Thou saidst: "I have a baptism wherewith I am to be baptised, and how am I straitened until it be accomplished!"[2] Thy heart, O Lord, was full of anguish and affliction, because the desire that Thou hadst was so great to see Thyself already dyed with Thine own Blood for love of us, that every hour that this was delayed seemed to Thee a thousand years, owing to the greatness of Thy love. And hence was derived that glorious Feast of Palms which Thou desiredst should take place when Thou wentest forth to suffer, in order to show the world the joy of Thy heart, since Thou

---

[1] Rom. ix. 3. [2] S. Luke xii. 50.

didst desire to go thus surrounded with roses and flowers to the bridal chamber of the cross. Thou didst not appear, O Lord, to be going to the cross, but to the betrothal, for it was such a festival that Thou didst desire to be celebrated on the way.

MEDITATION XVII.

ON THE EXEMPLAR OF LOVE WHICH THE SAVIOUR HATH GIVEN US IN HIS DEATH.

"GO forth, ye daughters of Sion," go forth, that is, ye devout souls of Jesus Christ, "and see King Solomon in the diadem wherewith his mother crowned him in the day of his espousals, and in the day of the joy of his heart."[1] I find no other garland, O Lord, than that which Thy Mother the Synagogue made for Thee on the Friday of Thy Crucifixion, one neither of leaves, nor flowers, but of cruel thorns to torture Thy Sacred Head. How then can this day be called a festival and the joy of Thy heart? Perhaps those thorns did not hurt Thee? They hurt Thee more than any amongst men, because Thy sensitiveness was greater; but because of the greatness of the love which Thou didst bear towards us, Thou didst not regard Thy pains but our healing, nor Thy wounds but the medicine for our diseased souls. If to Thy Patriarch Jacob the many years of his laborious servitude appeared but a few days so that he might marry Rachel,[2] because of the great love which he bore to her, what did those three hours on the cross and one

[1] Cant. iii. 11.   [2] Gen. xxix. 20.

day of Thy Passion seem to Thee that Thou mightest betroth Thyself unto Thy Church, and make her so beautiful that she should possess neither spot nor wrinkle?[1] This love caused Thee to die with such goodwill, it transported Thee in such a manner that it occasioned Thee to be stripped and suspended on a cross, and made the scorn and contempt of the world. O marvellous love! which didst descend to such an extremity, and singular blindness of men who took occasion to disbelieve Thee just when they had every reason to love Thee! Tell me, O most sweet love, if that mere spark which Thou hast shown to us here outwardly, was so wonderful to men as to become a stumbling-block to the Jews and foolishness to the Gentiles,[2] what would they have thought if Thou hadst shown them all the greatness of this love of Thine? What will Thy brethren, Thy sons and Thy friends who have such faith in Thee and such intimate knowledge of Thee, think when Thy love is more unfolded? This is what makes them beside themselves, remaining enraptured when, retired within the privacy of their hearts, Thou discoverest to them these secrets, and makest them understand and feel them. Hence arises their self-suppression; and the kindling of their affections; hence the desire of martyrdom; hence their contentment with tribulations; hence their delighting in what the whole world fears, their embracing what the world abhors. The

[1] Eph. v. 27. [2] 1 Cor. i. 23.

soul which is betrothed unto Thee, O Redeemer of the world, and which voluntarily unites itself to Thee in the bridal chamber of the cross, holds nothing to be more glorious than to bear within itself the offence of the Crucified. How then, my love, shall I repay Thee for this love? Blood must be repaid with blood. That blood which Moses[1] consecrated in cementing the friendship of God with His people by joining them in covenant with Him, and making an agreement with Him, and was the figure of Thy blood, was, in part, sprinkled upon the altar, and in part upon the people; that which fell upon the altar was in order to appease God; while that which fell upon the heads of the people was to impose obligation on men. Dearest Lord, I know this obligation; let me not abandon it; let me see myself bound by this blood and nailed to this cross. O cross! open a place for me and receive my body within thee, and deliver me to my Lord! Enlarge thyself, O crown, that I may be able to place my head within thee; O nails, quit those innocent Hands and pierce through my heart and wound it with compassion and love! For love of this kind Thy holy Apostle said Thou didst die to become supreme Lord of the living and the dead, not with menaces and chastisements, but with the deeds of love.[2] Account me, then, amongst those over whom Thou dost rule, either as living or dead, and behold me a captive under the sovereignty of Thy love. O

---

[1] Exod. xxiv. 6-8.   [2] Paraphrase of Rom. xiv. 9.

how wonderful and excellent a method of warfare hast Thou chosen, O Lord, since Thou hast conquered men not with a deluge, nor with fire from heaven, but with caresses of peace and love; not by slaying them, but by dying; not by shedding another's blood, but by giving Thine own for us upon the cross! O marvellous and novel virtue! for that which Thou didst not do for heaven when Thou wast waited on by angels, Thou didst upon the cross when associated with thieves! The tongues of fire which tell me that I should love Thee are as many as the wounds which I see and which Thou bearest in Thy Sacred Body out of love for me; every single wound amongst them is a tongue which cries out that I should love Thee. It will be well for thee, O my soul, to occupy thyself in loving Him Who at all times and in every place laboured with such great devotion to seek thee out. O greatness of Divine Love! inflame my whole heart that it may be completely filled with Thee, no other, lawless love finding place within me! O Paradise of the delights of God, and temple of peace for our soul, receive us wanderers and pilgrims in this valley of misery!

MEDITATION XVIII.

HOW THE CROSS OF CHRIST INFLAMES OUR SOULS WITH LOVE.

O STEALER of hearts, steal, O Lord, this heart of mine, for in the Scripture Thou hast the name of a robber, hasty and violent.[1] What sword shall be so strong? what bow so stout and well provided with arrows which could penetrate a fine diamond? The strength of Thy love has pierced an infinite number of diamonds. Thou hast broken through the hardness of our hearts; Thou hast inflamed the whole world with Thy love, as Thou hast said by a prophet: "With the fire of My jealousy shall all the earth be devoured";[2] in Thy Gospel Thou hast said: "I am come to send fire on the earth, and what will I but that it be kindled?"[3] Well did the holy prophet understand the efficacy of this coming and the value of this fire, when he cried saying: "O that Thou wouldst rend the heavens and wouldst come down, and that the waters would boil with the heat of the fire!"[4] O sweet fire! sweet flame which so kindlest the hearts that are more

---

[1] See Isa. viii. 3.   [2] Sophon. iii. 8, "igne zeli mei". Vulg.
[3] S. Luke xii. 49.   [4] Isa. lxiv. 1, 2.

frozen than the snow, and convertest them by love! This is the cause of Thy coming, to draw this fire down from heaven, and to fill the world with love, as the prophet says: "Thou hast visited the earth and hast inebriated it with love".[1] ["Thou hast visited the earth, and hast plentifully watered it: Thou hast many ways enriched it" (Douay).[2]] O most loving, gentle, beautiful, and merciful Lord, inebriate our hearts with this wine, kindle us with this flame, and wound us with this arrow of Thy love! What is wanting to this cross of Thine to make it a spiritual cross-bow since it so wounds our hearts? The cross-bow is made of wood and of a string stretched over, with a notch in the middle of it, where the string is fixed to despatch the arrow with great velocity, and to make a greater wound. Thus when Thy most sacred Body was extended on the wood of the cross, like a cord, and Thy arms also stretched out, I see that in the opening of thy side there was fixed as in a notch the arrow of Thy love that it might issue thence to wound the heart [of man]. Let the whole world know now that I have a wounded heart. O my heart! how shalt thou be healed? There is no remedy which will cure thee except death. When, my good Jesus, I see issuing from Thy side this

---

[1] Ps. lxiv. 10, "inebriasti eam" Vulg. The LXX. version conveys the same idea.

[2] The author makes use of the strong expression "embriagastella de amor"; an imagery employed by several of the ancient Fathers.

blood-stained spear-head,[1] and this spear is an arrow of Thy love which transfixes me, I feel that it wounds my heart in such a manner that there is no part left in it which it has not penetrated. What dost Thou desire to do, O sweetest love? What dost Thou wish to effect in my heart? I came there to be healed, and Thou hast wounded me; I came there that Thou mightest teach me to live, and Thou hast made me as though beside myself. O most sweet wound; O most wise frenzy! may I never find myself without Thee! Not only Thy cross, but the very form which Thou didst assume upon it, calls upon us sweetly. O loving Lord, and pure fire of love! Thou didst hold Thy Head inclined to one side in order to see us and to give us the kiss of peace, with which Thou didst invite the guilty, while it was Thyself Who wast the injured party! Thou didst hold out Thy arms to embrace us, Thy pierced Hands to bestow upon us Thy blessing; Thy opened side to receive us within itself; Thy nailed feet to wait for us, and that Thou mightest never be separated from us. So that beholding Thee, O Lord, upon the cross, all that my eyes discern invite me to Thy love. The wood, the form, the mystery, the wounds in Thy Body, and above all the love within Thee cry out to me to love Thee and never to forget Thee. How could I forget Thee? If I forget Thee, O good Jesus, let my right

[1] S. John. xix. 34.

hand be consigned to forgetfulness. Let my tongue cleave to the roof of my mouth if I do not remember Thee, and if I do not set Thee at the head of my joys.[1] Mark here, then, my soul, how the cause of the love which Christ bears to thee, is declared; for this love does not spring from a regard to anything that exists in man, but from Divine Love, and from the desire that possesses Him to fulfil the Will of God. By this means, then, thou canst understand from whence come such benefits and promises, as God has conferred on man, because thy hope is hereby strengthened by seeing upon what firm foundations it is based, and how the cause for which Christ loved man is not man himself but God; just as the medium through which God has promised such benefits to man is not man but Christ. The cause for which the Son loved us is because His Father commanded Him; and the cause for which the Father favoured us is because the Son besought Him, and merited the favour.[2] These are the super-celestial planets by whose marvellous appearance the glory of heaven is regulated, and they transmit all their influences and graces to the world. Dost thou perceive how firm are the pillars of love? Not less so are those of our hope. Thou lovest us, our Redeemer, because Thy Father commandeth it; and Thy Father forgiveth us because Thou entreatest

[1] Ps. cxxxvi. 5, 6, paraphrased and applied to our Blessed Lord.
[2] S. John xix. 30.

CHRIST'S CROSS INFLAMES OUR SOULS WITH LOVE. 101

Him to do so. From Thy seeing His Heart and Will it results that Thou lovest me, for so Thy obedience requires; and from His beholding Thy sufferings and wounds proceed my pardon and salvation, for so Thy merits demand. Ever thus behold them, O Father and Son, ever thus look upon them without ceasing, for thus will my salvation be brought about. O vision of sovereign goodness, O aspect of super-celestial planets, from whence proceed the rays of Divine grace with such certainty! When would such a Son disobey? When would such a Father not have respect to Him? If, then, the Son obey, I shall be loved; and if the Father regard the Son's merits, I shall be pardoned. Upon one aspiration which the maiden named Axa expressed to her father Caleb, her kind father granted her all that she asked of him.[1] What, then, could such a Father deny to the wishes and tears of such a Son? When, O my Redeemer, will the mire of my sins have such an ill savour that the sacrifice of Thy Passion would not swell more sweetly? So great is the beauty of Thy Sacred Passion that all the sins of the world joined together have no more part in defacing it than a very small mole in a countenance of great beauty and elegance. Then, O my weak and faithless soul, who in thy afflictions knowest not to trust in God, why is it that thy offences terrify thee? Observe that this affair does not depend upon thee but on Christ; because

[1] Jos. xv. 18, 19.

if the demerit of the first earthly man was the beginning of thy fall, the merit of the Second Heavenly Man was both the beginning and the completion of thy healing. Strive to be united to Him by faith and love, as thou art connected with the other by the bond of kindred; for, if thou shouldst be so united, then just as by the link of heredity thou partakest of the sin of the transgressor, so by the spiritual parentage thou partakest of the grace of Christ. If thou shouldst be united to Him in this manner, believe it as certain that that which belongs to Him shall be thine, and that which belongs to the Father shall belong to the sons, and that which is the property of the Head shall belong to the members, and, as the Gospel says, "Wheresoever the body shall be, there shall the eagles also be gathered together".[1] This is what David said figuratively of this mystery to a man timorous and perplexed: "Abide then with me, fear not; for he that seeketh my life seeketh thy life also, and with me thou shalt be saved".[2] Do not look to thine own strength, which will only cause thee dismay; but look to Him Who is thy Helper, and thou shalt acquire courage. Thus, if when crossing the river of life thy head becomes dizzy on beholding waters that are running past, lift up thine eyes on high and behold the merits of the Crucified One, and thou shalt pass over in security. If thou believest truly that the Father gave thee His

---

[1] S. Matt. xxiv. 28.   [2] 1 Kings xxii. 23 (altered).

Son, believe also that He will give thee the rest;[1] for all else is but little. Think not, my soul, that because He has ascended into the heavens thou art forgotten; for love and forgetfulness cannot agree together. He gave thee the greatest pledge of this when He ascended thither, *viz.*, the mantle[2] of His precious Flesh in remembrance of His Passion and Love. Observe that He did not only suffer for thee while living, but even after His death He received a portion of His wounds, *viz.*, the piercing of His side, in order that thou mightest know that both in life and in death He is thy true Friend; and that thou mightest understand also thereby that when He said, at the time of breathing His last, "It is consummated,"[3] although His pains were over, His love was not ended. "Jesus Christ," says S. Paul, "is yesterday and to-day and the same for ever;"[4] because such as He was in this world, while He lived amongst those who sought Him, such is He now and ever will be to those who seek Him.

[1] Rom. viii. 32.
[2] 2 Kings 4, 8, 13, 14.
[3] S. John xix. 30.
[4] Heb. xiii. 8.

MEDITATION XIX.

THAT GOD IS TO BE LOVED AS BEING OUR BENEFACTOR.

IF, as a heathen sage observed, we cannot repay the gods or our parents who only bestow upon us this hired house in which our soul resides, how much am I indebted to Thee, Thou true God and my only Lord, since Thou hast given me both soul and body and all that I am! Thou wilt draw me, as Thou sayest, with the cords of Adam, with the bands of love.[1] Those cords are the mercies which Thou hast bestowed upon Adam and his sons. Thou sayest herein that Thou wilt do such deeds for man that Thou wilt draw him to Thee. If to love means to desire the good of the person loved, how much must Thy love mean to me! If I wished to enter into a reckoning with Thee and to count up the blessings which I have received from Thy hand, the time would fail me and life would come to an end before such a protracted calculation could be concluded. As many members as I have in my body, so many benefits do I find on account of which I ought to love Thee. If one should lose an

[1] Osee xi. 4.

eye, how much would he love the Being Who should restore it! If one should deserve to lose his eyes, how much would he love Him Who should preserve them! Am I not bound then to love Him Who gave me my eyes and preserves them to me, though I have deserved to lose them many times for making a bad use of them? How much more am I bound to love Him Who raised me up when I was dead! O Creator of my life, restorer and preserver thereof! what do I possess in myself that I have not received from Thee? And, if it is so truly right that I should love Thee for the body and the life which Thou hast given me, wherefore should I not love Thee, and so much the more, for the reasonable soul which Thou hast created in me, since it is, beyond all comparison, of more value and excellence than this mortal and corruptible body of ours? and if this soul of mine should lose the use of reason, how much should I love Him Who should restore it! I am deeply bound to love Thee, since Thou hast given me the use of reason, a soul, a body, and life, and preservest them all, while I have many times deserved to lose them for my sins. Lift up, then, my soul, all thy thoughts to this unspeakable love of thy God. Nothing is more just, more useful, more salutary or more sweet, than that a man should love Him from Whom he has received his whole being and the preservation which he enjoys. If, my soul, thou canst not know what He is Who loves thee to such an extent, consider at least the pledges[1] which love has bestowed on thee. In the gifts which thou hast within thee thou wilt know with what affection and with what care and assiduity thou art bound to love. Thy pledges are conspicuous, thy gifts noble; it would therefore be unbecoming to make a paltry return for such great favours. Open thine eyes and behold the whole heavens, the earth, the air and all the elements and creatures which all do thee service. Thou receivest the benefit and dost not know Who it is that bestoweth it upon thee. If, then, my Lord, I fix my eyes on the treatment which Thou hast dealt out to me, I behold Thee, my God, so occupied in showing me mercies that it appears as if, forgetful of all the rest of mankind, Thou dost busy Thyself with me alone, and that Thou art taking care of me only.[2] Thou hast always been my solace in adversity and a guardian in my prosperity. Whichever way I wished to turn, Thy grace and pity went before me, and when I was on the point of being lost Thou didst deliver me. When I went astray Thou didst bring me back into the right way; when I was ignorant Thou didst instruct me; when I sinned Thou didst correct me; when I was sorrowful Thou didst console me; when I fell Thou

---

[1] "Arras" in Spanish are thirteen pieces of money which the bridegroom gives to the bride as a pledge in the act of marriage.

[2] So S. Augustine: "O Thou good Omnipotent, Who so carest for every one of us as if Thou caredst for him only; and so for all, as if they were but one!" (*Confession*, book iii., chap. 11, § 19).

didst raise me up and sustain me on my feet. Thou didst grant me to know Thee truly, to love Thee purely, to believe in Thee sincerely and to follow Thee fervently. O God of my heart, sweetness of my life and light of my eyes, dost Thou desire that I should love Thee? How shall I love Thee? and what am I that I should love Thee? How could it be that I should not love so generous a Benefactor, seeing how I am surrounded by His bounty? When the virtuous youth, Joseph, was solicited in Egypt by his immodest mistress, he called to mind the benefits he had received from his master, and answered her, saying, "My master hath delivered all things in his house into my charge, except thee, who art his wife; how then can I sin against my lord?"[1] He did not merely say, how should I wish to offend my lord? but, how could I do it? for it appeared to him impossible to injure one to whom he was so indebted. How, then, could I offend against Thee, my God, from Whose munificent hands I have received such benefits? Although my perverse will, with its liberty and its arrogance, sought to rid itself of Thy love, I know not how it were possible to offend against One to Whom I am so deeply indebted. If Putiphar entrusted his house

---

[1] "Contra mi señor," applying the word as if it referred to Pharao's officer, Joseph's master; whereas, according to the original Hebrew, the LXX. and the Vulgate, it really refers to God (Gen. xxxlx. 8, 9).

to Joseph, he did not make him lord over all of it, but reserved some part for himself, as he said. But Thou, O my Lord, what hast Thou that Thou hast not conferred upon me? In giving me Thyself Thou hast given with Thyself all blessings, and what do I possess that I have not received from Thee? Thus the remembrance of the benefits so numberless and exalted compels me to love Thee, so that even if I should wish to cease from loving, I should never be able to cease from doing so. The Paschal lamb, which Thou didst enjoin the Jews to celebrate,[1] and all the other festivals, were intended to recall to them the memory of the benefits which they had received from Thee. The Passover was the memorial of the going out of Egypt, and the offering to Thee of the first-born was the memorial of those first-born[2] children of their enemies whom Thou slewest in Egypt; the manna which Thou didst command them to preserve in the Ark of the Covenant was (as Thou didst Thyself declare) in remembrance of the food with which Thou didst sustain Thy people forty years in the wilderness; and the twelve stones which Joshua gathered out of the Jordan[3] were set up in order that the children of Israel might for ever remember the blessings that they had received when the river divided to afford a dry passage for them. In this and in the feast of

---

[1] Exod. xii.   [2] *Ibid.*, xvi.
[3] Jos. iv. 3, 6, 7, 20-24.

Tabernacles and in all other feasts and memorials which Thou commandedst them to celebrate, Thou hadst no other design than to cause the Israelites not to forget the mercies that Thou hadst shown them; that the memory of such supreme blessings should dispose their wills to love such a great Benefactor. When, in the Book of Deuteronomy,[1] Thou commandedst us to love Thee, before Thou didst set forth this precept, Thou saidst unto Thy people, "I am the Lord thy God Who brought thee out of the land of Egypt".[2] Thou didst set before their eyes the obligation which they were under to love Thee, recalling to their remembrance the benefits which they had received. All Thy gifts proceed from love, and thus Thou delightest, by the mercies which Thou bestowest, to bind us to love Thee, since there are so many reasons why Thou shouldst be loved by us.

[1] Deut. vi.   [2] *Ibid.*, v. 6.

MEDITATION XX.

THAT GOD IS TO BE LOVED FOR THE BENEFITS WHICH HE CONFERS UPON US.

IF gifts can break rocks, thou must be harder than a rock, my soul, if thou art not melted by the love of thy Saviour, seeing thyself so bound by the multitude of mercies which thou hast received and still receivest every hour. Dogs and all other irrational animals love their benefactor, and recognise and acknowledge the kindness which he shows to them. Why, then, should I, who am a rational creature and made in Thy image and likeness, be worse than the beasts by not loving Thee continually, my God and my Lord, since Thou never ceasest to constrain me by new and singular gifts? Thou hast complained, O Lord, of this ingratitude and thanklessness on the part of men, saying by Thy prophet Isaias, "The ox knoweth his owner and the ass his master's crib, but Israel hath not known Me, and My people hath not understood".[1] As it is natural for every living creature to love itself, and to endeavour to secure its preservation and its existence, so it is still more becoming to love him who does

[1] Isa. i. 3.

good to it; and this being a natural impulse in man, the apostle says that he who does kind deeds to an enemy heaps coals of fire upon his head,[1] by the love he thus enkindles. We read in the Scripture that David thus acted on two occasions towards his cruel enemy and persecutor Saul, whom by his kind conduct he converted to love.[2] O my perverse and hard heart! what great obstinacy is this that such countless benefits of thy God should not soften and melt thee into love for Him? O the forbearance and kind behaviour of David, how far do they fall short when compared with those of our Lord! Everything that Thou hast bestowed upon me was in order to oblige me to love Thee, and that I might give Thee my love. Thou hast served me, Thou Who art King of heaven and Lord of angels, in order to entreat me to repay love with love. O Lord my God and my supreme good, how much hast Thou done in order to be beloved by us miserable sinners! If Thou hadst given me permission to love Thee, it would have been a very great mercy and favour that Thou hadst done me, Thou being an infinite Majesty, while I am but a worm of the earth. How much greater the favour when Thou not only dost not disdain to be loved by me, but even solicitest my love with a multitude of gifts, so great is Thy Goodness and Clemency. Thou hast created me for love, and if Thou hadst not loved

---

[1] Rom. xii. 20.   [2] 1 Kings xxiv. 4-20; xxvi. 12-21.

me Thou wouldst not have created me. The cause of all things is Thy Will; and if Thou hast created me it is because Thou didst desire to do so; and Thou hast not only shown a most intimate affection in creating me, but an exceeding love in redeeming me. Though I owe Thee the debt of love because Thou hast made me, far more exceedingly do I owe Thee love because Thou hast bestowed a new being upon me by redeeming me when I was lost. When reduced by sin to a vile state of existence, and condemned to eternal fire, Thou didst restore me anew by means of a ransom, for which purpose Thou didst not send an angel nor a seraph nor a celestial spirit, but Thine own only-begotten Son, consubstantial with and equal to Thyself. O wondrous fervour of charity! O marvellous compassion! and singular example of love, which, in order to redeem a slave, made Thee send Thine own Son to die; and in order to endue with life a little worm of the earth made of clay did send down the Son of God from heaven to endure death! What was the cause of this? The great love which He had towards us and our race. Thou didst love me more than Thy earthly life, since Thou didst desire to die for me. Does it not appear to thee, my soul, that thou owest a debt of love to Him Who so loved thee? Does it not seem to thee that thou owest a tribute of love to Him Who loved thee before thou didst even exist? It is only just that thou shouldst pay to thy God this debt which is so deeply due. O Lord, I would ask Thy Divine Majesty, if I dared, why Thou, O Lord, dost love a thing so vile and a creature so useless as man? A master happens to have a slave very ugly and odious whom that master loves much; and if we ask this master why he fixes his affection on a thing so deformed he will reply that he loved him because that slave was very fond of his master and served him with the utmost attention and diligence. O Lord, shall I keep silence, or shall I speak? Truly I would be silent if just reason did not compel me to speak. Thou, O Lord, lovest this miserable slave, defiled by a thousand stains of sin; and while Thou art such as Thou art and he is such as he is, Thou dost not despise his abject condition, nor disdain to expend so rich a jewel as Thy holy love on so vile a thing. Thou lovest him, perchance, for what he has done for Thee? Dost Thou love him because he first loved Thee, or for his assiduous and fervent services? O sovereign Goodness and infinite Charity of my God, is it then so gratuitously, and only because Thou art Infinite Goodness, that Thou hast so deeply loved us and hast shown and dost still show by so many and such admirable deeds the stupendous love which Thou hast for us? And thou, my soul, if thou lovest a mere creature because he loves thee and has done something for thee, why dost thou not love thy

Spouse Jesus Christ, since He was beforehand in loving thee, and laid down His life for thee? If amongst the gifts of thy God this world is the least of all, how great dost thou suppose the greatest gift of all will be, since this which is the least is so great? He Who has bestowed gifts has imposed obligations, for we are under obligation to our benefactors. Men desire that not only should others acknowledge the good which they do when they are conferring any benefit, but they also desire acknowledgment for the good deeds which they have already done, and which they wish to be always kept in remembrance, so that when the gifts have ceased the obligation of the debt should not pass away. O exceeding good and great Lord, how great is Thy bounty and mercy, since Thou art satisfied with our loving Thee, when Thou art actually doing us good! Love thy God, then, my soul, when He sends thee gifts from heaven; and since thou receivest these pledges of love at all times from His most bounteous hand, it is most surely right that at all times thou shouldst love so munificent and noble a Benefactor. Love Him at least when He is doing thee good; and since He is always doing this thou oughtest always to love Him. All the different kinds of benefits, which are three, King David summed up when he said in the psalm, "Turn, O my soul, into thy rest, for the Lord hath been bountiful to thee. For He hath delivered my soul from death, my eyes from tears, my feet from falling."[1] All the benefits that we receive from any one are of three kinds, *viz.*, good things bestowed, evils from which he frees us, and blessings promised. The gifts which he received from God the Psalmist indicated when he said to his soul that it should return to God because of the benefits which he had received from Him. He treated of the second species of mercies when he said that God had delivered his soul from death and his eyes from tears. He performs a good work in our behalf who delivers us from any evil before we fall into it by admonishing us of the danger. He spoke of the blessings promised in saying that God delivered his soul from falling, promising him eternal glory and blessedness, wherein being confirmed in grace we shall see God, free from backsliding or falling into sins and offences; and in order to stimulate his soul the more that it may turn again unto God, he calls God his repose and rest, wherein he may refresh himself and enjoy relief from the toils and miseries which he endured while serving the world and his passions and appetites. It is, then, just and right, O my soul, that thou shouldst turn again to God, Who is thy rest and refreshment, from Whom thou hast received and every moment dost receive so many blessings; since, besides those gifts which He has bestowed upon thee, He has withdrawn thee from sins and delivered

[1] Ps. cxiv. 7, 8.

thee from hell, and has promised thee heavenly blessings. These three sorts of benefits thou oughtest to contemplate, going back over the past events of thy life, and drawing them forth from thy remembrance, acknowledging them to thy understanding, and representing them to thy will, in order that being inflamed with the love of so munificent a Benefactor thou mayest love and serve Him in accordance with the obligation wherewith thou art bound to Him. In these two verses of the Psalmist thou wilt find ample materials for contemplation concerning the innumerable mercies which thou hast received from God; so that shouldst thou not desire to love thy Creator as the *Summum Bonum*, infinite Goodness, and heavenly Beauty, thou mayest love Him, as though in spite of thyself, for the good things that He has done for thee.

MEDITATION XXI.

THAT GOD IS TO BE LOVED AS BEING OUR REST.

"TURN, O my soul, into thy rest,"[1] saith the royal prophet unto God. If to every man it is natural to love his own comfort and rest, then, O my heart, thou oughtest to despise the things of this world, and the affairs of time which hinder and disquiet one; and collecting thy thoughts, return to God and fix all thy care upon Him. O what rest and quietness wilt thou find if really closing the door against every other care thou wouldst place thyself in the hands of Jesus Christ, thy Spouse! There thy tears shall be wiped away; there shall cease the complaints which thou makest against the men who so disquiet thee; there shall all thy sorrows, vexations and toils be ended, and thou shalt find inward peace, joy of heart and paradise on earth. Thou sufferest many hardships, being perplexed and distracted by outward things, and while longing for rest dost not attain to it, though thou mightest find it without trouble. The dove of Noe[2] found no place to rest in outside of the ark, and so necessity compelled it to

[1] Ps. cxiv. 7.   [2] Gen. viii. 9.

return thither. Thou, O my dove, wilt not find rest out of the reach[1] of the true Noe, Jesus Christ: wherefore return to Him in Whom thy rest consists. In seeking peace elsewhere, thou forsakest thy God, to Whom thou *must* return if thou desirest to find what thou seekest. Thou must return to the same Being Whom thou hast offended, as the prodigal son did,[2] though thou dost not desire it. Jonas fled from God,[3] and in departing from Him, he found nothing but storm and tempest on the sea; but when converted returned to Him Whom he had forsaken, he found rest and a haven of safety. Agar[4] went out of the house of Abraham, her lord, and repaired to the wilderness, but the angel commanded her when she was spent with fatigue and hunger to return to the house of her master, Abraham, where she would secure life and refreshment. Leave then, my soul, this good and the other good, and return to Him Who is the true Good. Thou oughtest not to desire to love this or that good, that is to say, a finite and limited good, but love the infinite and unlimited Good. Do not seek this or that sweet thing, but seek and love that essential sweetness which subsists by itself. Thou must not love this or that beauty, but Beauty itself; nor this or that good thing, but the Supreme Good. If thou desirest true sweetness and delight, thou wilt not seek it in fruits

---

[1] Lit. "out of the hands".
[2] S. Luke xv. 20.
[3] Jon. i. 3 *seq.*
[4] Gen. xvi. 6, 7.

or in honeycombs, nor in bread or flesh, nor in any other food or other material resource whatever, but in the Delight and the Sweetness which exist in themselves and are dependent on none; a Sweetness not derived from anything else, but solely Sweetness itself in its entirety. And in the same manner, if thou seek beauty, seek it not in the sun or the moon or the stars, nor in man, nor in the heavens, nor in apparel, nor in gold or silver or precious stones, but seek it in Beauty itself; since that is not the beauty of this or that, but pure Beauty itself; which is not a medley of natural qualities, but is a Being of complete beauty, and is Sweetness, Goodness and pure Beauty, and so must needs be infinite and illimitable. Oh how will that abundance satisfy us, and how wilt thou, my soul, enjoy repose in that rest! Who could say, although he should be endowed with a hundred tongues and as many mouths, how satisfying that pleasure will prove, and how grateful that enjoyment! Oh how will that same gladness rejoice me, and how will that complete perfection of all goodness fill us with all that is good! If a honeycomb is delicious because of the sweetness which is in it, how much more so shall Sweetness itself be! If bread tastes of the flavour which is mixed with it, how much more will the flavour itself taste! If gold imparts delight by the beauty which the artificer has wrought in it, how much more will Beauty itself confer delight! Let who will boast himself and say that he has been labouring since the morning, bearing the burden of the day[1] and of the summer; let another praise himself, saying that he is not like other men, and that he fasts twice in every week;[2] yet Thou art very good to me, O Lord, to unite me to Thee, and to put my hope in Thee.[3] Let others trust in their sciences and the subtlety of their genius, in the nobleness of their blood, and in their dignities, honours and vanities of this life; yet I look upon all this as mere offal,[4] because Thou, Lord, hast been my hope, a tower of strength.[5] Let them fix their hope on the uncertainty of riches,[6] but I put my trust in Thy Word, for the love of which I have despised all things. Thou sayest that we should seek first the kingdom of God, and that all other things will be given to us.[7] "To Thee is the poor man left: Thou wilt be a helper to the orphan."[8] "If a battle should rise up against me,"[9] I will hope only in Thee, for Thou, Lord, art my rest, my refuge and my only good. O my soul, quit this and that good thing, and enjoy the Supreme Good itself, *viz.*, the true and real substance of goodness from which and through which springs all the good that there is. This is what thy God promises, and bestows on His friends and chosen ones, not rewarding them with any kind of good, but

---

[1] S. Matt. xx. 12. [2] S. Luke xviii. 11, 12. [3] Ps. lxxii. 28.
[4] Phil. iii. 8. [5] Ps. lx. 4. [6] 1 Tim. vi. 17.
[7] S. Matt. vi. 33. [8] Ps. x. 14. [9] *Ibid.*, xxvi. 3.

with Good itself and Bounty itself. Hence it is that when Abraham asked of God what He would bestow upon him in reward for his labours, the answer was returned to him, "O Abraham, all My bounty is given to thee".[1] This is to be the wages of thy work, and this the guerdon of thy labours. Turn thee again, therefore, according to the advice of the Psalmist, to thy rest; go back to thy God and Lord, for in Him alone shalt thou find in full perfection all that thou hast been continually craving by means of miserable and poor creatures. At least love thy God for thy peace and comfort, since in Him only is thy true repose.

[1] Gen. xv. 2 *seq.*

MEDITATION XXII.

OF THE BLESSING WHICH GOD BESTOWED UPON US IN GIVING US HIS SON.

AMONGST the innumerable benefits which we have received from Thy munificent hands, our God and Lord, that which holds the first place, and whereby Thou hast most clearly shown the boundless love which Thou hast towards us, consists in giving us Thy only-begotten Son. For, as Thy holy apostle says, "He Who gave us His Son, how shall He not with Him give us all other things?"[1] How will He deny to us what we ask of Him Who so freely surrendered Himself, and therewith gave us all blessings? and if the benefits received oblige us to love our Benefactor, I should begin to consider the abundance of good things which Thou hast conferred upon me that Thou mightest be loved by me, since Thou hast given Thyself for me, a gift which proceeds from the purest love, according to Thy saying to Nicodemus, "God so loved the world as to give His only-begotten Son for it".[2] This is the Supreme Good, the infinite

---

[1] An imperfect representation of Rom. viii. 32.
[2] S. John iii. 16.

Good, the most Divine, which Thou hast designed for us, in giving us Thy Son as a proof and manifestation of the ineffable love wherewith Thou lovest us. The medium and flowing fountain of infinite graces was the Incarnation of Thy Son our Lord Jesus Christ, by which He became man in our mortal and suffering flesh. This lesson I have to read with those eyes and that reflection wherewith Moses beheld the burning bush,[1] in which was depicted the working of this mystery; for just as the fire showed itself amongst the thorns of the bush without burning or consuming it, so to the Divine Person of Thy Son didst Thou unite our humanity without consuming it, though the fire of Thy Divine Love did burn therein. In fire also was that wonderful work revealed to Ezechiel;[2] for in the midst of the fire he beheld a form of Electron,[3] which is the finest gold of 20 carats, to represent the glory and excellence of our humanity, which shone with marvellous powers and wonders, and was exalted over every created thing. In the fire and in the midst thereof this mystery was revealed; for this Divine work flows from that Divine Fire of Love which Thou entertainest towards us; and so I have to consider it and try to approach it, as to a fire, in order to receive the warmth of Divine love which

---

[1] Exod. iii. 2.   [2] Ezech. i. 4, 27; xiii. 2.
[3] "Electro," a mixed metal of four parts gold and one of silver, much valued by the ancients.

overcomes the coldness of my heart. The more thoroughly I see into this lesson the more I find myself approaching the fire, whereby Thy holy love ought to increase in my breast, to burn there in living flames of the fire of love. Here my heart will halt and rest without passing on any farther, extracting Divine riches therefrom until I come to the end of my desires. The first living coal of love which is there given to me is to discern the time at which this mercy is promised to man, and the end for which it is granted to him. Amongst many other revelations made to the holy prophets who declared that Thou, O Lord, wert about to give us Thy only-begotten Son, one of the principal was that which Isaias uttered when Achaz[1] was king. That most impious king was placed in great distress, and Jerusalem was on the point of being destroyed, but Thou being desirous of relieving it, didst send the prophet Isaias with a message of comfort; and in order that he might be assured of the Divine promise the prophet gave the king the choice of selecting any sign whatever in the heavens or on the earth, by the fulfilment of which he would know that Thou wouldst truly deliver him, as the prophet told him, and that he should be freed from all the fear which possessed him. The wicked king understood that if he asked for any miracle in the heavens, such as that the sun should arrest his course or turn back-

[1] Isa. vii. 10, 11, 12.

ward, or that the earth should open itself, that God would be glorified and that His people would be converted to Him and would worship Him as their true Lord; and not desiring this result, but endeavouring to hinder it, he chose to continue in his fear and danger and to ask for neither sign nor miracle. Then Isaias lifted up his voice, and being full of zeal for the honour of God, said, "Do ye take it for a small thing to weary the servants of God by inflicting on them imprisonment, tortures and death, and was not this enough, but you must become the enemies and opponents of God in His own Person and Honour, obstructing the witness of His Divinity? Therefore, the Lord Himself shall give you a sign by which He will be much more glorified and exalted, far beyond all that this people could give of honour and praise. Behold! hearken and wonder, a Virgin shall conceive and bear a Son, Who shall be called Emmanuel, which signifies God with us." O wonderful word which affirms for what end this deed was done. What is this end, then? Why was it needful for God to become Man? Because man did not desire His honour and glory, and even endeavoured to hinder it though even at the risk of his own life. For love of man, Thou, my God, didst desire to impart the greatest of Thy gifts and to constitute it the greatest that man could receive, *viz.*, by giving him Thy only-begotten Son made true Man. From whence, O Lord, proceeds this great munificence which Thou showest to the world, but from that infinite charity and love of Thine, since the greatest of Thy gifts is promised in a season of sin and rebellion? What reason was there that the prophet should speak any more after man had desired to obstruct and impede the honour of God? Most certainly it would have been perfectly just that he should command the earth to open and that the workers of such wickedness should go down alive into hell; and yet this does not take place, but he promises that the heavens shall be opened and that God shall descend to the earth and should become true Man. So that if thou, my soul, dost consider the Incarnation of thy Spouse, Jesus Christ, as revealed by Isaias, and also contemplate it in reference to that moment when the first man offended his Creator, thou wouldst always find thyself in the midst of the fire of love. Adam offended the Divine Majesty,[1] and we with him; he hindered the honour and glory of God and our translation to the Paradise of His Kingdom without dying. Yet God did not deal with the question of our condemnation; but seeing that the counsel of His love concerning those who were to be saved was hindered, the Eternal Father offered His Son. Consider that God the Father said at the moment of Adam's transgression: Since thou settest thyself in opposition to the glory of those My creatures whom I so greatly love, I offer

---

[1] Gen. iii. 11, 22, 24.

My only-begotten Son that He may die and pay the penalty of this sin. He must become Man, not, as is consistent with the honour of the only-begotten Son of the Father, immortal and impassible; but I give Him that He may go in the form of a servant, like that which His brethren bear, that He may die and they may be saved.

MEDITATION XXIII.

OF THE LOVE WHICH GOD SHOWED TO US IN GIVING US HIS SON.

DESIRING to manifest to the world the great love which Thou hadst towards us, O most long-suffering and merciful Lord, Thy evangelist S. John writes that Thou didst so love it that Thou gavest Thy only-begotten Son for it.[1] The cause of Thy having shown to the world such singular mercy was no other than the great love which Thou didst feel, since it was love that made Thee give Thy Son. If we consider Who it is that loves, we shall find that he [S. John] says it was Thyself, my God, and the creature that Thou lovest is the world; and that which Thou givest to the world as a testimony of the love which Thou bearest towards it is Thy only-begotten Son. He Who loves is Thyself, O Lord, Who art God, the Supreme Good, infinite Beneficence, incomprehensible, ineffable and omnipotent, Whose centre is in every place, and Whose circumference or end is nowhere. For Thou, O Lord, Who art without beginning and without end, Who

[1] S. John iii. 16.

proceedest from none, and upon Whom all things are dependent and from Whom they receive their being, dost love the world. If the Evangelist had said that Thou didst love the angels, that would not have been any great matter, for of them the prophet declares that they are Thy ministers and servants, who do Thy Will.[1] If he had said that Thou lovest righteous men because they keep Thy commandments, we should not have been surprised at that; but it excites great wonder in us that Thou dost fix thine eyes on a rebellious world, the transgressor of Thy precepts, and that Thou lovest the world which is a violator of Thy Divine commandments; since He Who loves is God, and that which is loved is the world. Observe the difference and the inequality which one bears to the other—of God to the world and the world to God. Whoever speaks of the world speaks of weakness and sin, and this in Scripture signifies the world; and whoever mentions sin speaks of sinners, and whoever mentions sinners describes the enemies of God, and whoever speaks of the enemies of God speaks of those who are worthy of hell; and yet although He hates sin He loves sinners. O extraordinary and stupendous example of love! that God being what He is should love the world such as it is! For Thou, my God, being such and so great, art of such goodness that Thou dost not disdain to love a lost world, and to give Thy

[1] Ps. cii. 20, 21.

only-begotten Son as a token of the boundless love which Thou entertainest towards it. So thought Thy holy apostle when he said, in writing to the Romans, "God magnifies His love towards us in that while we were yet sinners He chose to die for us".[1] Thou magnifiest Thy love in loving men, and not only inasmuch as Thou lovest them but also in dying for them while they were sinners and Thine enemies. God so longed for us while we were His enemies that He delivered His Son unto death for our redemption and ransom. If we consider the extent of this love it is impossible to express it. "So greatly," says S. John, "did God love the world." How greatly? No one can possibly say the amount of this "how greatly" The degree of this love is certainly unspeakable, and so he had no words to express it, so that it is without limit or measure. When anything is so great that one cannot make it understood by means of words, the Scripture is accustomed to express it by the word "so". The great sorrow that the Holy Virgin suffered during the three days when she lost her only-begotten Son she betrayed in that word "so," when she said: "Son, wherefore has Thou done *so* to us?"[2] The weariness which the Lord felt when fatigued with His journey He sat down by the well near Sichar, and there came to Him a woman of Samaria, the Evangelist expressed in the words—"being

---

[1] Rom. v. 8, 9 (altered).   [2] S. Luke ii. 48.

wearied with His journey He sat down *so* [thus] on the well".[1] The great Divine power which the Redeemer showed when upon the cross with a loud voice He gave up His soul, S. Mark explained when he said, "Indeed this Man was the Son of God".[2] O Love, greater than heaven or earth, or all that God has created, since everything else is but a mere cipher in comparison with this love! This sovereign love, this boundless ocean and most profound sea of love wherewith Thou hast loved us, the Evangelist has comprised in that word " so " He *so* loved: He loved it so much and desired it so much, " that no one can tell the amount of this love, because He so loved that no one can either express or imagine the greatness of that love"; and the Evangelist, in order to declare the great love which Thou, my God, hadst towards the world, measures the love with the gift which Thou hast bestowed on us, which was so great that there is neither weight nor measure which can either weigh or measure it. Thou didst give us Thy only-begotten Son. That gift is equal to Thyself, and Thy pleasures, Thy essence, Thy existence, Thy goodness and riches. It constituted a gift as great as God Himself. The love, then, was as great as the gift. O Lord, Thou didst love the world with a love which was God. Dost Thou love us, O Lord, as Thou dost Thy only-begotten Son, since Thou gavest Him for us out of love? Who then is man

[1] S. John iv. 6.   [2] S. Mark xv. 39.

that Thou shouldst love him so? What kind of thing is man since Thou dost so magnify him and place him near Thy heart?[1] All flesh is grass, and all the glory thereof as the flower of the field and like unto vanity;[2] and yet with all this wretched man does not fail to offend his God, He being the God that He is, and man being such as you see. In order that no one should think that Thou didst love us with the heart only, or merely in words, the Evangelist points out the infinite character of the love which Thou didst feel for us by saying that Thou gavest Thy only-begotten Son for the world. Thou didst effect for the world all that Thou couldst do, and gavest it all that Thou couldst give. Abraham preformed many services unto Thee; for he quitted his country and his parents,[3] and as Thy apostle says, he believed, in hope and against hope, that Sarah could conceive; yet with all this, when he offered his son as a sacrifice, Thou didst so regard this service of his that Thou didst appear to forget all the past and didst say to him, "Now I know that thou fearest God, and hast not spared thy only-begotten son for My sake".[4] Abraham had served Thee well before this; but now Thou sayest that Thou knowest his goodness, because he laid his hands on the throat of his only son for love of Thee; for all the past did not reach to such a testimony of love

---

[1] Job vii. 17 (altered).   [2] Isa. xl. 6, xliii. 24 *seq*.
[3] Gen. xii. 1; Gal. iii. 6.   [4] Gen. xxii. 12.

as the delivery of his only son unto death for Thy sake. O my God, lover of our souls and sweetness of my life, now I know, my God, how much Thou lovest me, since for love of me Thou hast not withheld Thy only-begotten Son! Consider then, my soul, if these are true signs and most certain proofs of the infinite love which thy God bears towards thee. O bounty and liberality of God; for a Son Whom He had and that One so dear, God gave up for the world; He did not merely lend Him but gave Him! Thus said the prophet Isaias when speaking of the time at which He was given to us in His Nativity: "For a child is born to us, and a Son is given to us, and the government is upon His shoulder, and His Name shall be called Wonderful, Counsellor, God the Mighty, the Father of the world to come, the Prince of peace".[1] Thus God gave Himself in death to man, that He might confer upon man, through Him, that which He desired. This is what S. Luke relates, *viz.*, that the ruler Pilate, after having resolved to deliver to death the Author of life, gave Him up to the will of His enemies that they might do to Him whatsoever they pleased. Observe, O man, that thou art as much the master of God as of thy own property; and He is thine, and was surrendered up to thee so as not even to wish to die without obtaining thy permission. O inestimable work of love! since in order to bestow life on a slave He delivered His

---

[1] Isa. ix. 6

only-begotten Son unto death, and in testimony of the infinite love which He cherished for us gave us His Son, not lending Him but giving Him for us.

MEDITATION XXIV.

HOW GREAT WAS THE LOVE OF GOD IN GIVING UP HIMSELF.

O SUPREME and ineffable greatness of Thy charity towards men, my Lord! O wondrous fire of love! It is a marvellous thing that our hearts do not break with such great beneficence. For what else remained, O my Lord, after we had sinned but that Thou shouldst immediately cast us into hell like the angels who had displeased Thee? and if Thou, Lord, hadst chosen, Thou couldst easily have created another being much more noble who would have served Thee night and day. What kind of love was that which, when Thou wert insulted by our fall, prompted Thee to come and seek us with such solicitude? and after our sin didst desire to exalt us still more than before? Whence was this, when our sin was only deserving of great punishment? It all proceeded from the pure fire of love. That which most strongly moves my heart to love Thee is the profound consideration of the love that Thou hast shown to us. It is much more the fact of being loved than any benefits received which moves our love; for he who confers a benefit upon another person gives him some portion of what he possesses; but he who loves gives himself with what he has, so that there is nothing else left to give. Now then, O Lord, we may see whether Thou lovest us, and how great is the love that Thou bearest to us. Fathers greatly love their sons. Peradventure Thou lovest us as a Father? We have not entered into the intimate recesses of Thy heart to know this; but Thy only-begotten Son Who came down from Thy bosom, He brought us tidings thereof and commanded us to call Thee Father[1] for the greatness of the love which Thou bearest to us; and above all, told us that we should not call any other being Father upon earth,[2] because Thou alone art our Father; for as Thou alone art good by reason of the pre-eminence of Thy sovereign Goodness, so Thou alone art our Father, and Thou art so in such a manner and Thou doest such deeds to us that in comparison with Thy Fatherly affection no one else can be called father. Thy prophet was well aware of this when he said, "My father and my mother have forsaken and forgotten me, but the Lord hath taken charge of me".[3] Thou Thyself hast sought to compare Thyself with earthly parents, saying by the mouth of Isaias, "Can a woman forget her infant, so as not to have pity on the son of her womb? And if

---

[1] S. Matt. vi. 9; S. Luke xi. 2.   [2] S. Matt. xxiii. 9.
[3] Ps. xxvi. 10 (paraphrased).

she should forget, yet will not I forget thee. Behold, I have graven thee in My hands: thy walls are always before My eyes."[1] And because amongst the birds the eagle is most celebrated for loving its young ones, Thou, O Lord, choosest to compare with its love the greatness of Thine own love, saying, "As the eagle enticing her young to fly, and hovering over them, He spread His wings and hath taken him and carried him on His shoulders, the Lord alone was his leader, and there was no strange god with him".[2] Beyond this love of the bird is that of the bridegroom for the bride, of which it is said, "For this cause shall a man leave father and mother and shall cleave to his wife, and they two shall be in one flesh".[3] Thy love far surpasses this love, for, as Thou sayest by Jeremias, "If a man put away his wife, and she go from him and marry another man, shall he return to her any more?"[4] But thou hast committed adultery with as many lovers as thou hast chosen; yet withal return to Me, saith the Lord, and I will receive thee; and if, notwithstanding thou art still incredulous respecting such love, behold all the benefits which I have bestowed on thee, for all these are proofs and testimonies of love. Cast up the account of all these and see how numerous they are,

---

[1] Isa. xlix. 15, 16.   [2] Deut. xxxii. 11, 12.

[3] S. Matt. xix. 5.

[4] "To him," LXX.; "to her," Heb., Vulg. and Cipr. de Valera. Jer. iii. 1.

and thou wilt find that as many creatures as there are in heaven and earth, as many bones as thou hast in thy whole body, and as many hours and moments of life as thou hast, all these are benefits bestowed by the Lord; and mark also how many good inspirations thou hast received from the hand of thy God, and how many blessings thou hast enjoyed in this life, from how many sins has He delivered thee, and into how many infirmities and disasters thou mightest have fallen if He had not rescued thee; and that all these things are examples and tokens of love. Even the very calamities and tribulations which He sends upon thee are indications of love, for they are tokens sent from the heart of that Father Who scourgeth every son whom He receiveth,[1] in order to correct him, to awaken, to purify and to preserve him in all that is good. When threatening Thy chosen people Israel if they did not keep Thy commandments, Thou saidst by Thy prophet, "If his children forsake My law, and walk not in My judgments, if they profane My justices, and keep not My commandments, I will visit their iniquities with a rod and their sins with stripes".[2] Then to show that this chastisement was that of a loving Father, and that Thou wast not forgetful of Thy accustomed mercy, Thou didst add, "But My mercy I will not take away from him, nor suffer My truth to fail". And when, as a Father, Thou didst chasten Adam, casting him out of a

---

[1] Heb. xii. 6.   [2] Ps. lxxxviii. 31, 32, 33.

Paradise of joy, Thou didst provide him with clothing wherewith he should be protected from the heat of the summer and be sheltered from the cold of winter. O most clement and pitiful Lord, even in the troubles which Thou layest upon us, and even when Thou scourgest us, Thou dost display the great love that Thou hast for us! Then if I fix my eyes on this world, I see that it was all made for me, and solely for love of me, and that all things contained in it preach to me of love and denote love. And if thou, my soul, art deaf to all these things, that is no reason why thou shouldst be equally obtuse to the words which the Saviour speaks to thee in the Gospel, "God so loved the world as to give His only-begotten Son that whosoever believeth in Him may not perish but may have everlasting life".[1] All these things are tokens of love, and this still more so than all the rest, as the Evangelist S. John, who was so beloved by God and such a lover of Him, declares, saying, "By this hath the charity of God appeared towards us, because God hath sent His only-begotten Son into the world that we may live by Him";[2] and this blessing, together with the rest, are tokens of the love which God feels for us, and are like sparks that spring forth from that infinite and burning fire of love. How much greater, dost thou think, must be the hidden fire itself, since the very sparks that issue from it are so great? O infinite love! love profound and

[1] S. John iii. 16.   [2] 1 S. John iv. 9.

gracious, worthy of being requited with love. Grant us, O Lord, to feel with all the saints the height and depth, the breadth and length of this love, that our heart may be through its whole substance wounded and conquered by such great love.

MEDITATION XXV.

ON THE EXCELLENCE OF THE DIVINE LOVE.

THE charity with which Thou hast loved us, O most merciful Lord, is a virtue which in respect to the other virtues is like gold in comparison with the other metals. For just as gold exceeds every other metal in value, in estimation and in beauty, so doth Thy charity in perfection and excellence exceed the rest of the virtues, which if not enclosed[1] in charity possess little or no value. This Thy holy apostle expresses very well, saying: "If I speak with the tongues of men and of angels and have not charity, I am become as sounding brass".[2] The other virtues have no value without charity, and they all depend upon charity; yet it does not depend upon any other, but itself alone includes all virtues. It gives life to faith, securely trusts itself with hope, endures with patience, overcomes with courage, compassionates with pity, is silent with meekness, distributes with liberality, and finally exercises all the virtues; for, as the holy apostle says, it is patient,

---
[1] Lit. "*set* like a precious stone in gold".
[2] 1 Cor. xiii. 1 *seq.*

kind, is not moved by envy, doeth no evil, is not puffed up, seeketh not her own, doth not scoff at any one, thinketh no evil, rejoiceth not in iniquity but rejoiceth with the truth, beareth all things, believeth all things, hopeth all things, endureth all things. All these things are the natural fruits of other virtues which charity possesses united together, as experience shows us. In natural love and in that of the world, when one friend is very fond of another, he at once believes in him and trusts him with all he has, gives him all he can, and forgives him any offence or grievance that he has received. He feels no envy on account of the good things which the other possesses, endeavours to content him, does him no wrong, undergoes great trouble for the beloved object, encounters any danger; and the pain and grief which compassion for the other's suffering produces is greater than his own suffering. And so if that person by whose love he is captivated falls short in gladness, he feels excessive sorrow: if he fails in health, the friend is more afflicted; if he is poor, the friend is no longer rich; if he falls into adversity, the friend looks upon himself as a fellow-sufferer. If then worldly love acts thus in the case where it exists, how much more becomingly will Divine Love operate! O great influence and exceeding power and abundant energy of this holy Love! what thing is there that Thou canst not effect, however impossible it may appear? and what thing so difficult that

Thou canst not encounter, what thing so strong that Thou canst not overcome? O most mighty Love Who art strong as death,[1] and so much stronger than all strong things as Thou art more powerful than all powerful things, and as Thou art more sweet and gentle than anything in the world! O wondrous power of love, which not with iron, nor with weapons, nor with armed hand, but with a gentle sweetness and with sweet gentleness holdest all things under Thy sovereign sway, and in a wonderful manner constrainest the world to Thy service, and receivest tribute from all things. We know well, O Lord, how abundant, affluent and rich is Thy House, and how full of Divine riches. Amongst all Thy celestial treasures there are no greater riches, no greater treasure than Thy Holy Love; there is nothing more precious, nor more glorious, nor more to be desired. And since this is so, the greatest favour and benefit that Thou canst bestow upon a man is to give him Thy Holy Love. Let any one who desires it ask from Thee, my God, the gift of wisdom; let him ask the gift of prophecy; let him ask for humility and chastity, whatever he desires. I do not ask anything for myself except Thy Divine Love, for whosoever possesses that possesses all. This is the greatest blessing that can be desired, and the greatest boon that can be bestowed. And the reason is because whatever gift Thou grantest me, and whatever

---

[1] Cant. viii. 6.

benefit Thou condescendest to offer me, I hold of no account if Thou deny me Thy Divine Love, with which I attain to possess Thee, for love has such power that it causes Thee, Lord, to be mine, my possession and inheritance; and whosoever attains all that he can attain, yet if he does not obtain the love of God, does not secure the fruition of God. Divine fruition and Thy love are so intimately related [1] that there can be no fruition where there is no love. What then will it profit to possess all that one possesses, if we do not possess Thee, my God? For since Thou canst not confer upon us anything else of greater value than Thyself, so Thou canst bestow nothing more precious than Thy love, since with that Thou givest us possession of Thyself. If Thou shouldst give me the choice, I would sooner choose to love Thee without seeing Thee than to see Thee without loving Thee. For in not loving Thee, I could not possess Thee entirely, nor retain Thy friendship; while by loving Thee, although I might not see Thee, I could be Thy friend and could please Thy Divine Majesty, which without love is impossible. O Supreme Good! O Infinite Beneficence! give me Thy holy love, and make of me what Thou wilt. Have no fear, then, O my soul, because this chariot of Elias is of fire,[2] for it is the kindling of holy love that seizes upon souls and lifts them up to heaven. The children in Babylon feared it not, but

---

[1] "Están tan hermanados."   [2] 4 Kings ii. 11.

rather entered boldly into that fire, and while their bonds were consumed, they walked about free, singing and praising God with all creation.[1] This fire of holy love does not burn but gives light. Or we will rather say that it burns and does not burn; for in consuming the bonds it releases the prisoners from snares, annihilates tribulations and looses the chains of sin. But it does not singe even the hairs of the head of the just ones of God. Such is the power and might of the Divine fire of love, which, by purifying the desire of the flesh, spiritualises it, and exalts it to rejoice in Thee, O Lord, conjointly with the spirit, according to that which Thy holy prophet said: "My heart and my flesh have rejoiced in the living God".[2] It is a great thing to have subdued the flesh to so great a degree of spirituality, and to be so subject to the Spirit that it may rejoice together with the soul in God; but the great power of love can accomplish all that. Holy love anticipates the joys of the resurrection, when the spirit shall have entire dominion over the flesh, by subordination, even here, the body to the soul.

[1] Daniel iii. 25 *seq.*   [2] Ps. lxxxiv. 2.

MEDITATION XXVI.

OF THE BENEFITS OF THE INCARNATION.

THOU knowest well, O Lord, that likeness is a cause of love, and that there is no union of affection between two different subjects that are not in some respects alike. O infinite goodness of my God! what tongue could describe the things which Thou hast done in order to be loved by a vile worm of the earth such as I am? Thou didst bestow benefits without number upon man before Thy Incarnation, and didst visit him with innumerable gifts from heaven in order that, being allured by so many blessings, and seeing himself under such great obligations, he might fix his affections on so munificent a Benefactor; and seeing that all this did not secure his love to Thee, Thou didst desire to make Thyself like him and to become true man such as he is, in order that by this course Thou mightest gain his love. Before this there was great dissimilarity, and in many respects we were different and of distinct and diverse characters; for Thou, Lord, wast impassible, invisible, immortal, infinite, incomprehensible and eternal, while we are passible, visible, mortal, finite and limited, comprehensible creatures, temporal and earthly. But so unspeakable was Thy Charity and Love which Thou hast towards us that being such as Thou art Thou didst desire to be that which we are, by taking into Thy Divine Substance our human nature, being made man like us, mortal and passible, visible and resembling us, in order to be loved by us. And when it was necessary that for our redemption and life Thou shouldst absent Thyself from us, and after Thy death shouldst enter heaven and seat Thyself in our likeness at the right hand of the Father before removing from our eyes Thy bodily Presence, Thou didst, as a parting gift, institute the most holy Sacrament of the Altar, in order that, having Thy bodily Presence always before us, we should never be able to forget Thee. Thou didst appear in the world a true Man, being God in the likeness of sinful flesh;[1] in the sufferings which Thou didst endure in that nature, though not in guilt, from which Thou wast wholly free; like sinful flesh in the pains and death which sin brought into the world and which Thou didst endure without deserving them. In this way Thou didst overcome sin, and with it death, which entered into the world by it; as some one with the branches of a tree communicates fire to the tree itself, so that, as the apostle says, "from sin came the destruction and condemnation of sin".[2] O good Jesus, how much

[1] Rom. viii. 3. [2] *Ibid.*

more reason have we to sing Thy praises than the women who sang of the prowess of David,[1] who slew the giant with his own weapons! Thou, Lord, didst enter into the battlefield against the proud Evil Spirit, against whom no one had ventured, and with the staff of Thy cross and with patient endurance rather than with a stone, having concealed the weapons of Thy Divinity, Thou didst destroy him, cutting off his head with his own sword,[2] which are the effects of sin, *viz.*, pains and death. And thus Thou didst condemn sin in the flesh by giving Thy most holy Flesh to pains and death, whereby Thy honour was all the greater and the dishonour inflicted on the foe the more shameful. In this Thou didst show the great love which Thou bearest us and didst discover the treasures of Thy infinite wisdom, and hast manifested to the world Thy exalted power. When a knot is well made, the more its ends are strained, the more forcibly it is tightened. Thou, Lord, being God, didst so tie Thyself to our human nature that when death drew the ends together then the bond of love was tightened all the more, so as never more to separate; for that which Thou hast once taken upon Thee Thou hast never cast aside, but rather Thou hast manifested all the more the boundless love which Thou bearest to us. In this way those who once lay hold of Thee by love would sooner cast away

---

[1] 1 Kings xviii. 7.   [2] *Ibid.*, xvii. 51.

life itself and lose it than desert Thee or sacrifice Thy love. Lord, what couldst Thou do for us that Thou hast not done? Thou being inaccessible and heaven being closed to our sins, and not being able, through the weight of our offences, to reach Thee, Thou, Most Merciful Lord, hast designed to come to us in the lowliness of our flesh in order that we might be able to draw near to Thy Divine Majesty and enjoy Thy mercies. When a fierce bull stalks boldly and freely into the arena, few would dare to go near to him; but if he were afterwards tied and bound, any one who wished could approach him without fear. Before Thou wast incarnate, Lord, and didst invest Thyself with our mortality, no one dared to draw near to Thee, and for this reason Moses said to the people of Israel that no one should draw nigh to the foot of the mountain where Thou wast when Thou didst give the law, neither man nor beast, that they might not die.[1] Oza drew near and touched the ark of the Covenant and died immediately.[2] Nadab and Abiu, sons of Aaron, drew near, and were punished by sudden death.[3] King Ozias also approached the altar, and was smitten with leprosy.[4] Wherefore David speaking of Thee in the psalm, said, "Thou art the God to Whom vengeance belongeth".[5] But after Thou didst unite Thyself

---

[1] Exod. xix. 12, 13. [2] 2 Kings vi. 6, 7.
[3] Lev. x. 1, 2. [4] 2 Par. xxvi. 16-21.
[5] Ps. xciii. 1.

with our human nature and didst submit Thyself to the yoke of mortality by becoming Man, the Gospel declares that the publicans and sinners drew nigh to Thee, and that Thou didst eat with them.[1] Not only didst Thou not drive them away or put them to death, but rather didst receive them graciously, and mercifully forgave them their sins and lovingly consoled them. Do not fly, then, my soul; do not fly from thy Spouse Jesus Christ; for however foul and stained with sin thou mayest be, the Lord came down from heaven to the earth in the likeness of sinful flesh in order to wash away thy uncleannesses and to pardon thy offences. Who ever did so much for any bride as Christ did for human nature? If a very powerful king, becoming enamoured of a black captive, loved her so much as not only to ransom but even to marry her, would not that be exceeding love? And if, not content with this, he should desire to die for her transgressions, how much greater love would his love then be? O Spouse of my soul, Prince of Glory and King of Heaven, Thou hast done all this for me, for Thou hast loved me so much that Thou hast not only ransomed me, but, having been made Man, Thou hast betrothed Thyself in a Virginal Bride-chamber to human nature in an indissoluble marriage, and hast so exalted it that what is said of Thee in respect to Thy Godhead, that Thou art the Creator impassible and omnipotent,

---

[1] S. Luke xv. 1, 2.

may be also said of Thee as God made Man; and that which is said in respect of Thee as Man may be also said, by community of titles and names, of God, *viz.*, that He died, suffered and was buried; and Thy ineffable love did not cease here, since Thou didst desire to die for my sins and offences. Aaron and Mary [Miriam] murmured against their brother, Moses, because he had married an Ethiopian woman.[1] What would they have said, then, if he had died for her? But Thou, O Lord, didst not only give Thyself to us in Thy most holy Incarnation to be made Man, but wast willing to lose Thy life upon the cross in order to bestow life upon us.

[1] Num. xii. 1.

Made in the USA
Coppell, TX
01 December 2024

41448061R00089